Basic English for Science

Teacher's Book

D0183208

Oxford University Press

Oxford University Press, Great Clarendon Street, Oxford OX2 6DP

Oxford New York
Athens Auckland Bangkok Bogotá Buenos Aires Calcutta Cape Town
Chennai Dar es Salaam Delhi Florence Hong Kong Istanbul Karachi
Kuala Lumpur Madrid Melbourne Mexico City Mumbai Nairobi Paris
São Paulo Singapore Taipei Tokyo Toronto Warsaw

and associated companies in
Berlin Ibadan

ISBN 0 19 457180 7   student's book
ISBN 0 19 457181 5   teacher's book
ISBN 0 19 457189 0   class cassette
ISBN 0 19 457188 2   language laboratory cassette set
ISBN 0 19 457187 4   class tape
ISBN 0 19 457186 6   languange laboratory tape set

Oxford and Oxford English
are trade marks of Oxford University Press

First published 1978
Seventh impression 2000

Basic English for Science was researched, developed and written
by Peter Donovan at the Oxford University Press English
Language Teaching Development Unit.

Printed in China

contents

introductory notes

aims of the course

Basic English for Science is designed to help meet the language needs of
non-native speakers of English who are preparing to study a science
subject for which English is a medium of instruction. It aims to develop a
basic range of expression in English which will enable the student to deal
with the concepts used in the teaching of science, and in scientific
discussion and writing.

The course presupposes a minimal knowledge of English, and may be
undertaken by students who have recently begun a first course of study in
English of a more general kind, or who have followed a secondary school
course with weak results. It is designed to lead the student towards an
intermediate level of English. The book may, of course, be used as the
basis of a course of study for students who already have some knowledge
of English, possibly up to intermediate level, but who now need to
orientate their study towards the English used in relation to scientific
subjects. The book would then also serve the purpose of a refresher or
remedial course which was directly relevant to the student's language
needs.

background

The term 'science' embraces a very wide area of subject matter, and
different students of science will have widely differing interests within the
many subdivisions of this field. This presents a problem when preparing
students for the language they will need to study different branches of
science. It is therefore necessary to establish some common element in the
language used in physics, chemistry and biology and their associated
disciplines.

A basic introductory English course cannot teach all the specialist
terminology and vocabulary peculiar to each branch of science. However,
what is common to the many branches of science is a **method** of scientific
thought and enquiry. This method of enquiry involves the student in
various **language operations.** A student in any of the sciences will need to
be able to use different combinations of these language operations
according to the activity being carried out. Examples of these operations
are *describing* (shape, size, attributes, construction, operation, position,
etc) ; *predicting, hypothesizing, speculating on cause and result, accounting
for observed results, concluding,* and so on.

A student carrying out an experiment, for example, may have to follow
spoken or written instructions and then write a report of the experiment
when it is completed. In doing so, the language operations of describing
the apparatus, how it was set up, the reactions or results observed,
explaining the results and concluding will usually be needed. Other
activities will involve different combinations of such operations, and the
student may need to be able to recognize these in the spoken and written
language.

Mathematics forms a basic common element in most scientific study,
and students of science need to be able to deal with numbers and
mathematical formulae. This may involve the student in understanding and
producing the spoken English forms of equations, numbers, abbreviations

and symbols, although this skill is not usually taught in English courses for foreigners.

This course therefore aims to develop the student's ability to handle a range of basic language operations, and the ability to read, reproduce and understand numbers, formulae, numerical values and units in spoken English.

design

The course is designed with the aim of developing the student's ability to express in English the concepts involved in studying a science subject. The language content and the ordering of the material in *Basic English for Science* therefore departs from more traditional English courses. This is quite deliberate, as the starting point has not been made from the point of view of a grammar syllabus, but from the need of the student to perform and recognize the language operations outlined above. The structures, vocabulary and expressions taught in the course follow directly from placing the communication needs of the student first.

Some of the structures presented would be found in most English courses, but in this course they are taught because they perform a function in a particular language operation. For example, the modal verb *should*, which in a more traditional course might be introduced at one point as part of a system of modal verbs, is presented in two units: in Unit 6 as one linguistic form of the language operation of giving instruction (*The experiment should be repeated . . .*), and in Unit 8 in the language operation of expressing likely result (*The wood should burn, provided it's dry . . .*).

For this reason there are also omissions from the range of language which is normally found in a basic English course. This is because the course concentrates specifically on the English required for performing language operations in the context of science. Where a structure or usage can be covered in the context of general English and is thought to be well catered for in terms of teaching material already in use, this item has not been included in the course. For example, the language items *for, since,* and *ago* are usually presented and drilled in basic English courses in the context of general English. It does not seem that these items have a particularly specialized function in terms of the language operations developed in this course. *For* is probably the most common in this context (*The solution was shaken for several minutes*), but this usage is very similar to that presented in general English courses, and no overt teaching point is made of it here. *Since* and *ago* seem to be even less specific to a science context, and although they may occur in statements such as *I've been working on this experiment since lunchtime* and *I took a reading five minutes ago*, these usages are in effect those usually covered in a general English course and are not related to particular language operations in the sense used here.

scientific content

The scientific context in which the language operations are presented includes as wide a range of interest and relevance as possible. An understanding of certain phenomena is necessary as a basis for the study of most areas of science. Topics such as the structure of the atom, basic electricity and electrochemistry, and an understanding of the nature of solutions, acids and alkalis, the classification of matter, materials, forces and pressure are some of the areas which have a general relevance throughout the sciences. In addition to such topics, the course also makes use of everyday processes such as opening a cylinder lock or striking a match, which require the student to think logically and use English to produce clear, simple explanations and descriptions.

The emphasis throughout the course is therefore placed on the expression of basic concepts in clear, simple, acceptable English. The actual scientific material which forms the context for this development is kept as simple as possible, referring wherever possible to everyday examples. In this way, any bias towards a particular specialization within the field of science is avoided. The emphasis throughout the course is placed on the expression of concepts through the structures and vocabulary in various language operations. The course can therefore be taught by a teacher who does not have a background in science.

Students who already have a background in one or more of the sciences should find that many of the topics covered are familiar to them. This should enable them to concentrate on the various ways of expressing scientific concepts in English. In addition, students who are at the beginning of their study of science should find much in this course which relates directly to their study, together with material which can be easily understood purely within the terms in which it is presented in this course. There should be no need for outside reference in order to explain the material in the course and cope with the language exercises.

For this reason, the teacher using this course will be concentrating more on the language aspect than the scientific content of the material. The examples from science used in the course should be clear enough for the teacher to use without a detailed knowledge of the subject. Where it is thought the teacher may need guidance or some explanation, this is given in the teacher's notes.

language activation

The language activity which a student of science studying in English will be involved in must obviously vary according to the nature of his study. English may only be required in order to have access to reference material in written form, or it may be the medium of instruction and of communication between the student and his contemporaries. Courses in English for science have in the past placed a great deal of emphasis on the study of written science texts. Whilst these have a large part to play in the study of science, it is clear that in many situations the ability to communicate effectively in spoken English and to understand spoken discourse on science topics is at least as, if not more, important.

The range of possible language skills required of a student will be evident if consideration is given to the activities involved in situations such as understanding a lecture, understanding the classroom presentation of a topic, taking part in the classroom discussion of a topic, carrying out laboratory work, understanding a textbook, following instructions, writing up an experiment, and so on.

The precise emphasis which a student requires on particular combinations of skills will be determined by the nature of the language activity. This will therefore vary with different groups of students. *Basic English for Science* has been designed to give a great deal of practice in developing the ability to communicate in clear, simple, spoken English, to understand spoken English in a context of science, and at the same time to develop the ability to understand and produce written English in the field of science.

structure

The course consists of:

Student's Book   Containing all the exercise material needed by the student, including instructions and notes for language laboratory drills.

Teacher's Book   Containing notes and keys for the teacher, suggested class activities, oral drills and guidance for using the material. The Teacher's Book also contains scripts of all recorded material.

Language Laboratory Tapes   A set of six tapes, containing the Drills. These are available either as cassettes or on open reel.

Class Tape   Containing a selection of the material from the Classwork sections. These include dictation material on formulae from the earlier units and a selection of the material from the Classwork sections of the Student's Book. The tape has been produced to serve two main functions:

1   as a reference tape for the teacher, particularly to give guidance in the pronunciation and stress of expressions which might be unfamiliar;
2   as a tape for use in the classroom to provide a native speaking model or to relieve the teacher of having to read a text several times.

Parts of the Classwork which are included on the Class Tape are marked with the symbol ⊗ in the margin of the Teacher's Book. The extracts are identified on the tapes by their unit number, section number and letter heading (A, B, C, etc). The Class Tape is available either as a cassette or on open reel.

contents

The course is divided into eleven units, the first ten of which are organized in the following way:

classwork (three sections)   This consists of outline diagrams, charts, drawings, examples of structures, etc, in the Student's Book. The student completes these during or after the teacher's presentation of new teaching material in the classroom. When these have been completed by the student they provide a written and visual record of what has been covered in class.

The Teacher's Book provides the material to be presented to the class, guidance on its use and keys to class exercises.

exercises (three)   The three exercises correspond to the three sections of Classwork. The exercises may be completed by the student working alone after the appropriate Classwork section has been covered (Exercise 1 after Classwork Section 1, etc). They are designed so that throughout the course the student is guided towards a freer use of language in his writing.
   The Teacher's Book contains the key to these exercises.

drills (six)   There are two drills for each of the three Classwork sections. They often depart from the more familiar type of drills in that many of them require the student to combine material presented in the Student's Book in the form of diagrams or tables with the prompt heard on the tape. In this way the responses elicited are as meaningful as possible.

activity   This is designed to activate the language practised in the Classwork and Drills in a more open-ended situation, the teacher providing the guidance for the activity. Guidance and prompt material for these activities are given in the Student's Book and in the Teacher's Book.

   Unit 11 is a revision and test unit, and may be used for either of these purposes according to the wishes of the teacher. The drills in this unit are designed to test aural comprehension as well as speaking ability. There are no Exercises in this unit, as all of the Classwork can also be done by students working individually if desired.

organization and use of the course

The course begins with developing the ability to read, say and understand numbers, units and simple arithmetical processes. It then progresses through describing simple shape, giving dimensions, basic geometry, expressing spacial relation, describing more complex shape, etc, until by Unit 10 the student should be able to follow all the stages of conducting an experiment, from understanding a series of instructions, following an explanation, to writing a report of the experiment.

timetabling

Each of the Classwork sections is designed to occupy approximately two forty-five minute teaching periods. This may, of course, be varied by the teacher by spending more or less time on particular aspects of each section. It should, however, be possible to complete one Classwork section in a double lesson (one hour thirty minutes). In addition, the Activity will probably occupy at least one further classroom lesson when all three Classwork sections have been covered. The Drills would normally occupy about three periods in the language laboratory (two drills per forty-five minute period). Exercises can be done in the student's own time, but the teacher may wish to correct these in class time.
   A suggested path through a unit would therefore be as follows:

CLASSROOM   LANGUAGE LABORATORY   PRIVATE STUDY

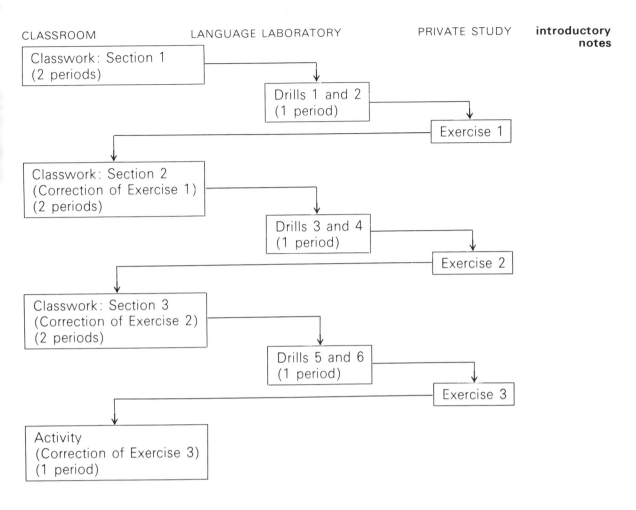

TOTAL CLASSROOM TIME=7 PERIODS

TOTAL LANGUAGE LABORATORY TIME=3 PERIODS

This arrangement may not of course be possible from a timetabling point of view, in which case it may be varied, bearing in mind the relationship of the various components outlined in the section **structure.**

handling the course

Detailed notes and guidance for handling each stage of the Classwork in each unit are given in the Teacher's Book. However, a general technique for handling these sections may be suggested here.

In the earlier units in particular, the teacher is usually advised to begin presenting the language activity in each Classwork section while the students have their books closed. For example, in Unit 1, Section 1, the activity of practising reading and recognizing numbers around the class is suggested. The students open their books after this has been begun, and the material in that section is then used as a basis for extending the activity. In this way it is hoped that students' attention is focused on the language operation to be developed rather than on the printed page at the

introductory notes

initial stage. That is, the material should form the basis for the active use of language in meaningful situations.

In later units, students will sometimes need their books open at the beginning of the presentation of a Classwork section, in order to make use of the printed material, but wherever possible the teacher is encouraged to use the visual aids suggested in the notes and present the situation as realistically as possible in the classroom. For example, in Unit 10, Section 1, the discussion of what happens as a result of mixing sand and water and sugar and water would be made much more meaningful if the experiment were actually performed in the classroom.

The Activity in each unit often requires the teacher to provide objects and materials which are readily available. The language activity here will generally be freer than in the Classwork sections, and the teacher should be prepared to guide students in their use of the language practised in the preceding parts of the unit, correcting, interpreting, and supplying any necessary vocabulary and expressions. The aim here should be to place the students in a situation in which there is a need to communicate meaningfully, so that the relevance of the language taught becomes apparent in the context. Students will obviously not be able to express themselves with perfect grammatical correctness throughout this exercise. The teacher should not try to correct every mistake, as this is not the aim of the Activity.

teaching 'kit'

Since the teacher is often called upon to supply various objects for use in the Classwork and in the Activity, it is suggested that a 'kit' of basic materials is built up. This might include a collection of measuring equipment for use by the students (such as rulers, tape measures, etc) and simple objects with which shape, size, attributes and construction may be demonstrated. This kit may then be used throughout the earlier units. It might include boxes in assorted shapes and sizes, balls and objects in the shape of cones, cylinders, pyramids, and so on, together with an assortment of objects made of different materials and in different colours.

acknowledgement

The authors and publishers would like to thank all those teachers and institutions who used this material in its draft and pilot stages, and who made corrections and suggestions for its improvement. In particular, the period of testing and evaluation of the material at the Colchester English Study Centre was an invaluable part of the development of this course.

unit 1

classwork

SECTION 1 **numbers and dimensions**

With *students' books closed*, present and practise how to read numbers, with particular reference to the following points:

0	*nought, oh* (*zero* is not often used in reading decimal values)
1–10	
11–19	*eleven, twelve, -teen*
20–99	*twenty one, -two, -three* etc
100–999	*nine hundred and ninety-nine*
1,000–999,999	(comma to denote thousands)
1,000,000	*one million/a million*

Write numbers from all of these groupings on the board. Point to different ones at random, asking individual students to read them. Present the method of reading decimal values: 35·395 is read: *thirty-five point three nine five*, not: *thirty-five point three hundred and ninety-five*. In Britain the decimal is always represented by a point: 12·00 and not by a comma: 1,000 which is reserved for thousands.

When these have been thoroughly drilled, students open their books.

 A Individual students read values from the table, for example:

teacher	*Number one*
student	*Three*

When these have been practised, present the ordinal numbers *first* to *twentieth*. Ask individual students: *What's the (third) number in the table?* etc, at random. Then ask: *Which number is (73·5)?* Students answer: *The (sixteenth)* etc.

 B Read out the following values. Instruct the students to write down the figures with a comma or a decimal point according to the values heard. For example, *If I read the first figure as eight point five nine three, you write 8·593*.

Values:

85·93	27,149	385·293	00·100	10·301
91,349	72,835	3·005	28·1	7,219

C Ask students if they know how to read the abbreviations:

mm	*millimetre*
cm	*centimetre*
m	*metre*
km	*kilometre*

Make sure they can say these correctly (repeating in chorus if necessary). They should be able to recognize the terms and write down the abbreviations.

Students should write down the full names of the units in C.

D Read out the following values, which the students should write down. For example, *Number one: twenty millimetres.*

1	20 mm	5	19·28 cm	9	108·35 cm
2	3·2 cm	6	0·035 cm	10	1,732 cm
3	538 km	7	2,375 km	11	15·023 cm
4	28·32 cm	8	70·2 m	12	76,394 m

With *students' books closed*, present the words: *height/high, length/long, width/wide.*

Use objects around the classroom (tables, desks, etc) and objects you supply (boxes, pieces of wood, etc) to present these terms. Present the corresponding question form: *How high/long/wide is ...?*

Get individual students to measure various objects, giving dimensions: *It's ... cm high/long/wide.*

Present the question form: *What's the height/length/width of ...?* Ask the students these questions about the objects they have measured. Get them to ask each other the questions. Students then practise using this question form, asking about the dimensions of the various objects.

E *Students open their books* and copy down the words *height, length* and *width* with reference to the diagram in **E**. In brackets, the words *high, long* and *wide* should be written down.

Point out that the words *broad* and *breadth* are sometimes used instead of *wide* and *width.*

F Students use the tables as prompts for asking about the dimensions of objects. Point to various objects, or write a list on the board, to act as a cue for a student to ask a question. Get students actually to measure things where possible, using rulers, tape measures, etc. For example, teacher pointing to desk:

student 1   *How high is the desk?*
student 2   *It's 70 cm high.*

If desired, the word *about* may be introduced to allow students to give approximate dimensions without having to measure every object. For example, *It's about 1·5 m long.*

Point out the distinction between *height, width, breadth* and *length*, which are nouns, and *high, wide, broad,* and *long*, which are adjectives. (A simple distinction at this stage is that we can say *the height*, but *high* is used alone.)

When some work has been done as above introduce approximate values by using: *It's approximately/roughly/nearly/almost/just under/just over ... It's between ... and ...*

Explain that *height, width* and *length* are linear dimensions. Students note this down.

After sufficient practice, carry out similar drilling with students' books closed.

G Students make a table with *wide, long, broad* in the adjective column, and *width, length, breadth* in the noun column.

Students should be told to add to this list as they meet new noun/ adjective pairs.

H This is an oral exercise in stating dimensions. Each set of dimensions 1, 2 and 3 is taken in turn and questions are asked and answered about the dimensions of the block. There are various possibilities for conducting this exercise:

1   The teacher asks individual students *What is the height ... ?* etc.
2   The teacher indicates pairs of students to ask and answer *What is the height ... ?*
3   The teacher asks *Which dimension measures 2·75 m?* Students answer *The length.*

Repeat the exercise, getting students to give approximate dimensions. For example, *It's nearly 3 m long* etc.

SECTION 2   describing objects

With *students' books closed*, select various objects to illustrate the meanings of the terms *thickness, depth* (*thick* and *deep*), *hollow, solid, internal, external*. Present also the names for the parts of a circle:

c = circumference
d = diameter
r = radius

and the adjective *circular* or *round*. (*Round* being used more in general rather than scientific contexts.)

A *Students open their books* and note down the appropriate terms from those just presented, with reference to the drawings. It is best for these to be copied from the board, so that spellings are noted correctly. The statements should be as follows:

1   *thickness*
2   *depth*
3   This object is *solid.*
4   This object is *hollow.* h is an *external* dimension. d is an *internal* dimension.
5   The adjective to describe a circle is *circular* or *round.* A circle has dimensions of *diameter, radius* and *circumference.*

The noun/adjective pairs introduced here should be added to the tables the students began in Section 1.
The question forms: *What's the (height) of ... ?* and *How (high) is ... ?* should be revised, and then applied to *thick, thickness, deep, depth* with

students asking and answering questions about objects. For example, *What's the thickness/depth of … ? How thick/deep is … ?*

Introduce also the question form: *Is … hollow/solid?* with the answer: *Yes, it is.* or *No, it isn't, it's solid/hollow.*

B Demonstrate how simple descriptions of objects may be built up, as in the examples. Substitute other dimensions for those given (5 cm, 4 cm, 10 cm) and get students to make similar statements.

Descriptions of objects 1–5 may then be built up as a class exercise, asking individual students to give descriptions, with the rest of the class correcting or approving the descriptions. These may be written on the board, then erased at the end, leaving students to write their own descriptions. Alternatively, students may write descriptions or copy them from the board during the exercises.

Words which will be needed to complete the descriptions are:

1   *block/side (B is a cubic wooden block of side 8 cm …, etc)*; 2   *plate*; 3   *disc*; 4   *tube*; 5   *block/strip/beam/girder.*

These words may be given to the class before doing the exercise, or supplied during the exercise when students need to use them. The exact wording of each description may differ, but each one should conform to one of the patterns in the examples.

C Check that students know the words: *square, triangle, rectangle (oblong), ellipse, semicircle,* by asking: *What's the first shape called?* etc.

Students should note these down. They should also know the corresponding adjectives: *square, triangular, rectangular (oblong), elliptic(al), semicircular.* (*Oblong* is used more in general English than in scientific contexts.)

The adjectives of shape are then used to complete the descriptions of objects A to E.

1   Object A is a *square* plate of side *5 cm* and *thickness* 0·01 cm.
2   Object B is a *triangular* plate of side *18·7 cm* and *thickness* 1·2 cm.
3   Object C is a *rectangular* plate having a *length* of 15 cm, a *width* of 3 cm and a *thickness* of 0·5 cm.
4   Object D is an *elliptical* plate of *thickness* 2·1 cm.
5   Object E is a *semicircular* plate which has a *radius* of 3·5 cm and a *thickness* of 0·05 cm.

The Alphabet
If students are having difficulty recognizing the letters of the English alphabet, conduct some drill work on this area, as from this point onwards the ability to understand and produce spoken letters in formulae, labels and spelling becomes extremely important.

If necessary, practise individual and chorus repetition of each letter. Test students at random around the class on recognition and production of letters written on the board.

Write some familiar initials on the board, eg BBC, EEC, UN, etc, and discuss their meaning. Insist on acceptable pronunciation. Introduce the expression: *What does … stand for?*

D Present the names of the three-dimensional shapes illustrated:

A cube cubic cuboid
B pyramid pyramidal
C sphere spherical
D ellipse ellipsoidal

E cone conical
F hemi-sphere hemi-spherical
G cylinder cylindrical

Ask the following two types of questions:

What's A/C/E called? It's a cube/sphere/cone and
What shape is A/C/E? It's cubic/spherical/conical.

Choose letters at random rather than proceeding in sequence.

Students then make statements about the objects illustrated, using names of materials as modifiers. For example, *A is a metal cube. E is a solid copper ellipsoid.* The names of the materials may need to be explained.

E This part may be conducted as a class exercise. There are various possibilities, eg,

1 Students write down descriptions as in the example.
Students' efforts are corrected/discussed together, and a correct version evolved.

2 Students are asked individually to give oral descriptions of the objects. Then the teacher writes these on the board, and students copy them either one at a time or all together after completing the series of descriptions.

The words *ball, cup, empty, flask, tube* may need to be introduced.

F By means of the diagrams or by using suitable objects, explain the meanings of the following adjectives:

1 *curved*
2 *flat*
3 *rounded*
4 *pointed* (also: *sharp* when referring to cutting ability)
5 *straight*

6 *curved*
7 *dotted*
8 *broken*
9 *zigzag*
10 *wavy*

These words may be presented by asking students to try to complete the statements orally and writing down the appropriate words (the teacher supplying the appropriate word where necessary). *Or:* Present the words first, using objects and drawings while students' books are closed, and then ask the students to complete the statements, first orally and then writing down the words.

Before going on to **G,** make sure students know the following words. If necessary, present them using suitable visual aids such as boxes, blocks etc.

top
bottom/base

side
end

edge
corner

G Demonstrate, with reference to visual aids and objects in the room, how descriptions can be built up using the adjectives in **F** together with these nouns. For example: *The top of the table is flat. It has rounded corners.* And so on.

With students' books open, use the illustrations in **G** to conduct a class drill. Ask individual students: *What shape is the end of P?* They answer: *It's pointed*, etc.

This can be extended as follows:

teacher   *Describe P.*
student   *It's got/It has a pointed end.*

After some teacher–student questioning, get students to ask you and ask each other similar questions.

Note that Z is a contrast between *sharp* and *blunt* as well as *sharp* (or *pointed*) and *rounded*.

SECTION 3   describing shape, size, use, etc

Students' books closed. If possible, supply a variety of objects of different shape, size, weight, colour, use, etc for this activity. Try to select objects whose shape can be described with the language already taught. Have some objects which have other things inside them, and some which consist of more than one part (eg a matchbox containing matches and consisting of a tray and a sleeve).

A *Students' books open.* This is a class exercise in simple physical description. The basic patterns which can be used for asking questions and making descriptive statements about things are set out in the tables.

The activity may be started by taking each aspect of description in turn, and describing a number of objects as fully as possible according to each aspect (eg first shape, then size, then colour, etc). It may start with the teacher asking questions, but should involve students asking and answering each others' questions as soon as possible.

Where an exact description is not possible with existing vocabulary, exploit the modifiers which are given, ie *roughly, more or less, nearly, almost*, etc. Present the use of *light* and *dark* to modify colour.

Proceed to fuller descriptions of individual objects, with students trying to describe objects as fully as possible according to size, shape, weight, colour.

Use suitable objects (pens, rulers, chalk, keys, etc) to present the structure:

What's it used for?
It's used for ——ing (something)

example (with a matchbox):
It's used for holding matches/keeping matches in.

Present also:
    What's it **made of**?
    It's **made of** wood.

    What does it **consist of**?
    It **consists of** an inner tray and an outer sleeve.

    What does it **contain**?
    It **contains** about 50 matches.

B *Students' books open.* Students should use the patterns as set out in the tables to make similar questions and statements about other objects such as those in the illustrations.

When sufficient practice has been given with books open, students should close their books and continue asking questions and making statements. Indicate an object and then select two students to ask and answer:

teacher   *X ask Y about the shape of this.*
student X *What shape is it?*
student Y *It's roughly (circular).*

Go round the class so that as many students as possible are required to ask a question about a single object. Do not allow the same question to be repeated about the same object.

C Using the table together with suitable objects and drawings, present the concept of **opposite.** For example,

teacher   *This is curved, but this is . . . ?*
student   *Flat.*

Present the structure: *What's the opposite of . . . ?* (Write the pattern on the board). Point to various objects/drawings and ask: *Is this flat?* Students reply: *No, it isn't, it's curved* and so on with various pairs of opposites.

Use this drill to introduce the following opposites:

long/short   regular/irregular
strong/weak   empty/full
thick/thin

These pairs can be added by students to the list given in their books. The list, with these additional items, can be copied into their notebooks.

Use the drawings for students to ask and answer similar questions. Indicate pairs of students to ask and answer.

D Show how general statements describing things can be built up using the language covered so far, as in the examples.

Draw attention to the way the indefinite *a* is used to refer to a class of things. For example, *a pencil* meaning *pencils in general*, *a match-box* meaning *match-boxes in general*.

Also involved here is the way information can be added to give a more complete description, using the defining relative clause with *which*. The sentences illustrate a very common pattern in scientific and technical English.

The descriptions of objects can be carried out as a class exercise, with students reading out the descriptions using *which*. The descriptions with *which* are then written into their books when the teacher has corrected the oral versions.

Some words may need to be explained before or during the exercise. These are: *eraser/erase, strip* (eg *a strip of wood/paper* etc), *draw, compare, sealed, tall*.

1   An eraser is a solid block of rubber which is used for erasing pencil marks. It can be either rectangular or round.
2   A ruler is a thin rectangular wooden or plastic strip which is used for drawing straight lines and measuring linear dimensions.
3   A standard mass is a solid cylindrical brass block which is used for comparing masses on a laboratory beam balance.
4   A laboratory thermometer consists of a sealed hollow glass tube with a spherical bulb at one end which both contain mercury. A thermometer is used for measuring temperature.
5   A beaker is a hollow cylindrical glass container which is closed at one end. It is used for holding liquids or solids.
6   A measuring cylinder is a tall hollow cylindrical glass container which is closed at one end. It is used for measuring volumes of liquids.
7   A test tube is a short hollow glass tube which is rounded at one end. It is used for holding liquids or solids.

E Provide the class with a series of three (or more) objects, which can be described in the simple terms of shape, size, colour, material, weight, and use etc, which the class has already practised.

Suitable everyday objects are: pencil, eraser, matchbox, cigarettes, cigarette box, ash tray, cardboard box. Simple laboratory apparatus may be used if available.

The students can then be presented with each object in turn, or they may be allowed to choose three objects from those presented. They then write down brief details under each of the headings for objects 1, 2 and 3.

The students may be allowed to ask for help, consult each other, or be made to produce their own descriptions, as the teacher wishes. The descriptions are then discussed and compared by the class together.

exercises

exercise 1

1 The block has a *height* of *9·35 cm*, a *length* of *11·52 cm* and a *width* of *2·01 cm*.
2 The *length* of the block is *11·53 cm*, the *width* is *3·28 cm*, and the *height* is *0·05 cm*.
3 The block is *23·01 cm wide*, *112·35 cm long* and *18·9 cm high*.
4 How *wide* is the block?
  What's the *length* of the block?
  How *high* is the block?
  What's the *width* of the block?
  How *long* is the block?

exercise 2

1 A is a *solid cylindrical* steel *bar*, of length 39·1 cm and *diameter* 9·3 cm.
2 B is a *hollow* copper *tube* having an *internal diameter* of 21 cm, an *external diameter* of 55 cm and a *length* of 93·2 cm.
3 C is an aluminium *block/beam/girder* which has a *depth* of 21·2 cm, a *thickness* of 0·5 cm, a *width* of 30 cm and a *length* of 100 cm.
4 The cone D has a *height* of 88·5 cm, and a *base diameter* of 23·0 cm.

The following answers may be varied slightly.

5 E is a solid rectangular wooden block of length 84·2 cm, height 9·8 cm and width 23·4 cm.
6 F is a solid plastic strip of length 1 m, width 0·03 m and thickness 0·005 m.
7 G is a curved iron bar of length 0·75 m, height 0·08 m and thickness/ width 0·05 m.
8 H is a solid (circular) porcelain disc of diameter 12 cm and thickness 0·5 cm.

exercise 3

Individual students' drawings will vary and therefore need to be checked separately.

drills

drill 1

1   What's the first value?
    Thirteen centimetres.
2   What's the second value?
    Twenty-eight point five centimetres.
3   What's the seventh value?
    Nine hundred and thirty-five point two oh one centimetres.
4   What's the twelfth value?
    Fourteen point one four metres.
5   What's the ninth value?
    Seven hundred and twenty-three point five eight metres.
6   What's the sixth value?
    Ninety-eight point oh two one centimetres.
7   What's the eighth value?
    Oh point oh nine one five kilometres.
8   What's the tenth value?
    Five point oh oh two centimetres.
9   What's the fourth value?
    Seven point three eight five metres.
10 What's the fifth value?
    Eight thousand seven hundred and twenty point five kilometres.
11 What's the eleventh value?
    Thirty point three five centimetres.
12 What's the third value?
    Five hundred and thirty-four point eight kilometres.

drill 2

1   What's the height of the block?
    The height is twenty-eight point five one centimetres.
2   How wide is the block?
    It's thirty-two point oh eight centimetres wide.
3   How long is the block?
    It's seventy-three point two nine centimetres long.
4   How high is it?
    It's eight point three two centimetres high.
5   What's the width?
    The width is seven point nine three centimetres.
6   What's the length of it?
    The length is twenty-four point three four centimetres.
7   How high is it?
    It's ninety point oh five centimetres high.
8   What's the width of it?
    The width is eighty-eight point nine five centimetres.
9   What's the length of it?
    The length is two hundred and twelve point oh oh centimetres.

10 How high is it?
    It's nought point three one centimetres high.

11 How wide is it?
    It's nought point four five centimetres wide.

12 What's the length of it?
    The length is two point seven two centimetres.

drill 3

1 What is **A**?
   A is a circle.

2 Is **F** square?
   No, F isn't square, it's cubic.

3 What is **C**?
   C is an ellipse.

4 What is **F**?
   F is a cube.

5 Is **G** a curve?
   No, G isn't a curve, it's a straight line.

6 What is **H**?
   H is a sphere.

7 Is **D** a straight line?
   No, D isn't a straight line, it's a wavy line.

8 What is **I**?
   I is a curve.

9 Is **B** a rectangle?
   No, B isn't a rectangle, it's a triangle.

10 What is **E**?
    E is a cylinder.

11 What is **A**?
    A is a circle.

12 What is **H**?
    H is a sphere.

drill 4

1 What's the depth of **M**?
   Thirty-two point four three centimetres.

2 What's the radius of **P**?
   Twenty-two point three centimetres.

3 What's the height of **N**?
   Fourteen point four centimetres.

4 What's the length of **L**?
   Twenty-five point three three centimetres.

5 What's the internal diameter of **O**?
   Seventy-six point three centimetres.

6 What's the height of **K**?
   Three point oh five centimetres.

7   What's the width of **Q**?
    Fourteen point nine centimetres.

8   What's the external diameter of **O**?
    A hundred and twenty point four centimetres.

9   What's the length of **Q**?
    Seventy-three point oh five centimetres.

10 What's the height of **Q**?
    Eight point one centimetres.

drill 5

1   Is **R** pointed?
    Yes, it is.

2   Is **T** flat?
    No, it isn't, it's curved.

3   Is **X** empty?
    No, it isn't, it's full.

4   Is **T** curved?
    Yes, it is.

5   Is **W** light?
    No, it isn't, it's heavy.

6   Is **Y** regular?
    No, it isn't, it's irregular.

7   Is **U** rounded?
    Yes, it is.

8   Is **Z** hollow?
    Yes, it is.

9   Is **V** curved?
    No, it isn't, it's straight.

10 Is **S** straight?
    No, it isn't, it's wavy.

drill 6

1   What is it?
    It's a thermometer.

2   What's it used for?
    It's used for measuring temperature.

3   How long is it?
    It's twenty-four point four centimetres long.

4   What's the external diameter of the bulb?
    One point three five centimetres.

5   What's the external diameter of the tube?
    Nought point four nine centimetres.

6   What's it made of?
    It's made of glass.

7   What does it contain?
    It contains mercury.

8   What's the internal diameter of the bulb?
    Nought point nine nine centimetres.

activity

Students are told to choose an object which they can describe simply. They may be allowed to choose from any in the room, or alternatively the teacher may have a number of objects concealed from the class. One student at a time is then allowed to examine one object, without the rest of the class being able to see. Each student then writes down a description of his particular object under the appropriate headings. (If the class is relatively small—around ten students—then each student could be provided with an object in a box. The student examines the object without the others in the class being able to see it.)

When all of the class have written down their descriptions, each student in turn is 'cross-examined' by the rest of the class, who ask questions such as *Is it large?*, *Is it heavy?*, etc. The student may only answer *yes* or *no*. When a *yes* is scored, the teacher writes up the appropriate words on the board, eg *very heavy*, *blue*, *plastic*, etc. As the description is built up, the class tries to discover what the object is. This is repeated with as many students' objects as possible, a score being kept of the number of objects the class manages to guess correctly. (It should be pointed out that if the descriptions are accurate, the class should be able to guess the object fairly easily.)

During this activity, the class may well require words and expressions of description which have not so far been taught, and it is up to the teacher to use his discretion as to how much further vocabulary students are able to cope with at this stage, although the students' need for new vocabulary in order to communicate ideas should result in a greater receptiveness to new vocabulary and expressions. The teacher should therefore be ready to help students with words and phrases if they get stuck in their descriptions.

unit 2

classwork

SECTION 1   **describing angles and lines**

A With *students' books closed*, introduce the terms *horizontal* and *vertical* (eg with simple blackboard work). Introduce the expressions: *a horizontal line, a vertical line, at right angles to* (as in: *the wall is at right angles to the floor*), *perpendicular to*. A *right angle* is an angle of 90°, and in geometric convention is denoted in this way:

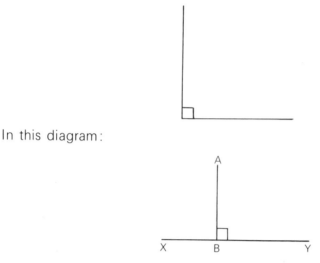

In this diagram:

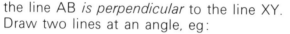

the line AB *is perpendicular* to the line XY.
Draw two lines at an angle, eg:

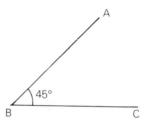

and explain that this can be described in English in three ways: *AB̂C is a forty-five degree angle, AB̂C is an angle of forty-five degrees, AB is at an angle of forty-five degrees to BC*. Draw other angles and get students to make similar statements.

   Students open their books and complete the descriptions of the lines and angles.

1   This line is vertical (a vertical line). This line is horizontal (a horizontal line).
2   The line AB is perpendicular to the line XY. AB̂Y is a right angle.
3   EF is at an angle of 45° to FG.
4   HÎJ is a 95° angle. HÎJ is an angle of 95°. HI is at an angle of 95° to IJ.

B Students use the different expressions introduced and noted in **A** to describe the angles in this exercise.

The teacher asks: *How big is angle DEF? What's the size of angle JKL? Describe the angle PQR, Which angle is 50°?* and so on.

Students may ask and answer questions in pairs about the angles.

The sign ' represents *minutes*, so that 130° 12' is read as *a hundred and thirty degrees, twelve minutes.*

C The three main types of angles are identified. Draw them on the board and elicit or present the names before students write them down. (The sign < is interpreted as *less than* and > is interpreted as *greater than*.)

An angle less than 90° is called an *acute angle*.
An angle greater than 90° is called an *obtuse angle*.
An angle greater than 180° is called a *reflex angle* or an *external angle*.

Students should then be asked to describe the angles in **B** according to these classifications.

D Students and teacher together identify the different types of triangles.

ABC is an *equilateral* triangle.
DEF is a *right-angled* triangle.
GHI is an *isosceles* triangle.
JKL is an *obtuse-angled* triangle.
MNO is an *acute-angled* triangle.

E Either by drawing diagrams on the board, or by using those in the book, present the following geometrical terms:

AB and CD are *parallel* lines.
FG is a *diagonal* line.
IK and JL are *intersecting* lines.
Lines IK and JL *intersect* at X.
The line PN *bisects* the angle MNO.
PN is the *bisector* of the angle MNO.
The line XZ *bisects* the line QR at Y.
The line XZ is the *bisector* of the line QR.

F Get students to describe the figures as fully as possible. Suitable model answers would be:

DÊF is an acute angle of 25°
GHIJ is a rectangle of length 25 cm and width 10 cm, which has/with a diagonal GI.
The acute angle KLM is bisected by the line LN.
The line QR bisects the line OP at right angles.
ST and UV are parallel lines of length 15 m.

Instruct students to draw figures such as:

A square ABCD with a diagonal BD.
A right-angled triangle.
An acute angle.
An obtuse angle.
Two intersecting lines.
Two parallel lines.

SECTION 2 **reading basic formulae**

With *students' books closed*, write up simple arithmetical expressions on the board. See if students know how these are read in English. For example: $2+2=4$

> Teacher *How do we read this in English?*
> Students *Two plus two equals four.*
> Teacher *What's the name for this arithmetical process?*
> Students *Addition.*

Students may well need to be taught the words: *plus, minus, times, divided by* or *over* (as in $\frac{a}{b}$: *a over b*), *addition, subtraction, multiplication, division*.

Illustrate these terms with other simple sums on the board. Get different students to read these out individually.

Dictate some simple sums and get students to write them down, with the answers. For example, *What's 4 plus 7 plus 9 minus 12?* Get students to read back the sums, with answers. Write them on the board as students read them back. Dictate some simple formulae in a similar way. The following may be used:

$$a+b+c=x$$
$$d-e+y=z$$
$$\frac{ab}{x}=0$$

$$7y-8b+c=12$$
$$\frac{1}{x}=\frac{1}{y}$$
$$7ab=9-b$$

Introduce the words *brackets* for the sign ( ) and *square brackets* for [ ]. Illustrate with these examples:

> a minus b in brackets times a plus b in brackets equals y.
> a open brackets 7−b close brackets equals x.
> 12 plus a minus b in brackets all over 7a equals b.
> x open square brackets a minus b in brackets times a plus b in brackets minus 7 close square brackets equals nought.

$$(a-b)(a+b)=y$$
$$a(7-b)=x$$
$$\frac{12+(a-b)}{7a}=b$$

$$x[(a-b)(a+b)-7]=0$$

Erase these examples and dictate them to students (in a different order). Get students to dictate them back while you write them on the board for correction.

Present the distinction between **capital letters** (*A, B, C, D,* etc) and **small letters** (*a, b, c, d,* etc) which are important in reading many formulae. In general, the distinction is not usually made unless the two types occur in the same formula. For example: $Ft=mv-mu$.

A *Students open their books.* They should be asked to speak these formulae. They may write down how the formulae are spoken, as below:

$a+b=c$ *a plus b equals c*
$a-b=d$ *a minus b equals d*
$a\times b=e$ *a times b equals e*

$\dfrac{a}{b}=f$ a over b equals f

$a \times b=e$ a multiplied by b equals e

$\dfrac{a}{b}=f$ a divided by b equals f

Students should copy out a table of nouns and verbs used for mathematical processes in the following way:

sign	noun	verb
+	addition	add
−	subtraction	subtract
×	multiplication	multiply
÷	division	divide

The signs ( ) are called *brackets* (we say *open brackets, close brackets*, or *a+b in brackets*).
The signs [ ] are called *square brackets*.
ABC are *capital letters*; *def* are *small letters*.
R_x is read *R subscript x*.

B With *students' books closed* outline the system for reading fractions in English. Write up the following fractions on the board, and ask: *How do we read this fraction?* Explain that they are called fractions. Get individual students to read them out at random, as you point to different fractions. Add further 'regular' fractions.

$\frac{1}{2}$ a half
$\frac{1}{4}$ a quarter
$\frac{1}{3}$ a third
$\frac{3}{4}$ three-quarters
$\frac{2}{3}$ two-thirds

The remainder of the fractions are regular in their formation:

$\frac{1}{8}$ an eighth
$\frac{3}{16}$ three-sixteenths

And so on, adding *-th(s)* to the appropriate figure.
    Students open their books and practise reading these fractions. They should copy them into their notebooks and write down their spoken forms for reference.

C   Using the conventions outlined in **A**, it is possible to read a large proportion of the formulae a student will encounter in English. The formulae in this section are all taken from genuine examples, and the students may recognize some of them. They should not, however, concern themselves with their meanings, since this exercise aims to develop the students' ability to produce and recognize spoken forms of simple formulae. Students practice reading these formulae aloud.
    There may be slight variations in the way these can be read, but the

most generally acceptable forms are set out below. The capital/small letter distinction is usually only made when both forms are used in the same equation. $\frac{d}{dz}$ is a convention for the process of differentiation.

1 x equals a plus b all over c
2 x plus y equals capital A over a minus b
3 I equals a plus open brackets n minus one, close brackets, d
4 capital V equals capital I capital R
   (or simply: V equals IR, since this is a well-known formula for electricity)
5 one over u plus one over v equals one over f
6 v equals u plus at
7 capital F times small t equals small m small v minus small m small u
8 one over capital R equals minus capital M over capital E capital I
9 d capital Q over dz equals minus q
10 capital E equals capital T plus capital P minus small c plus small e

D The values are read as follows:

x^2	*x squared*
x^3	*x cubed*
x^n	*x to the power (of) n, or x to the n*
x^{n-1}	*x to the power (of) n minus one, or x to the n minus one*
x^{-n}	*x to the power (of) minus n, or x to the minus n*
$\sqrt{x}$	*square root of x*
$\sqrt[3]{x}$	*cube root of x*
$\sqrt[n]{x}$	*nth root of x*

Write each one on the board, asking: *How do we read ...?*
Write down the full spoken version, which students copy down.
Practice them rapidly at random around the class.
   The values in the second table should also be practised around the class. Students will need to be familiar with their pronunciation.

E The expressions here, which should be practised around the class, are somewhat more complex than those in **B**.

1 x to the power of minus p equals one over x to the power of p
2 x to the power of p over q equals the qth root of x to the power of p
3 x squared minus a squared equals x plus a in brackets times x minus a in brackets
4 y equals a times e to the power of kx
5 x equals nx subscript one plus mx subscript two, all over m plus n
6 y minus y subscript one equals y subscript two minus y subscript one, all over x subscript two minus x subscript one, all in brackets, times x minus x subscript one all in brackets
7 x squared over a squared plus y squared over b squared plus z squared over c squared equals one

8   *d* equals the square root of, open square brackets, open brackets, *x* subscript one minus *x* subscript two, close brackets, squared, plus, open brackets, *y* subscript one minus *y* subscript two, close brackets, squared, plus, open brackets, *z* subscript one minus *z* subscript two, close brackets, squared, close square brackets

9   *b* squared equals *a* squared, open brackets, one minus *e* squared, close brackets

10 *x* squared plus *y* squared plus two *gx* plus two *fy* plus *c* equals nought

SECTION 3   **reading more complex formulae**

With *students' books closed* build up the following table on the board, writing up one symbol at a time and asking if students know what it means in English. Write in its meaning and write up an example, getting students to read the example aloud. When the table is completed, students should copy it down.

symbol	meaning	example	spoken
$\equiv$	equivalent to	$x \equiv y$	x is equivalent to y
$\neq$	not equal to	$x \neq y$	x is not equal to y
$\simeq \doteqdot \approx$	approximately equal to	$x \doteqdot 10$	x is approximately equal to 10
$\rightarrow$	tends to	$x \rightarrow 0$	x tends to nought
$<$	less than	$x < 5$	x is less than five
$>$	greater than	$x > 5$	x is greater than five
$\ll$	much less than	$y \ll 5$	y is much less than five
$\gg$	much greater than	$y \gg 5$	y is much greater than five
$\leqslant$	less than or equal to	$x \leqslant 10$	x is less than or equal to 10
$\geqslant$	greater than or equal to	$y \geqslant 10$	y is greater than or equal to 10
$\propto$	proportional to	$x \propto y$	x is proportional to y
∞	infinity	$x \rightarrow \infty$	x tends to infinity
$\pm$	plus or minus	$x = \pm 2$	x equals plus or minus 2
$\therefore$	therefore	$\therefore x = 0$	therefore x equals nought
$/$	per	km/hr	kilometres per hour

A The numbered signs and symbols in the students' books may then be used for practising and testing students' grasp of these.

B The names for the Greek letters may be elicited from the class if they are known, or they should be presented by the teacher. The accepted British English pronunciation is as follows:

alpha	/ˈælfə/		nu	/nju/
beta	/ˈbitə/		xi	/ksaɪ/
gamma	/ˈgæmə/		omicron	/əʊˈmaɪkrən/
delta	/ˈdeltə/		pi	/paɪ/
epsilon	/epˈsaɪlən/		rho	/rəʊ/
zeta	/ˈzitə/		sigma	/ˈsigmə/
eta	/ˈitə/		tau	/taʊ/
theta	/ˈθitə/		upsilon	/jupˈsaɪlən/
iota	/aɪˈəʊtə/		phi	/faɪ/
kappa	/ˈkæpə/		chi	/kaɪ/
lambda	/ˈlæmdə/		psi	/psaɪ/
mu	/mju/		omega	/ˈəʊmigə/

(Reference: A. S. Hornby, *Oxford Advanced Learner's Dictionary of Current English.*)

When they have been introduced, the letters should be practised at random around the class.

C The expressions should be read out as follows. Individual students should practise reading them.

1 *f* equals one over two pi times the square root of *LC*
2 *E* equals sigma *T* to the power of four
3 Capital *W* subscript *s* equals two pi small *f* over capital *P*
4 Gamma equals *W* subscript oh over four pi *R* all times *F*
5 Mu subscript oh equals four pi times ten to the power of minus seven capital *H* small *m* to the power of minus one
6 *C* equals *L* over *R* squared plus omega squared *L* squared
7 *v* subscript two equals the square root of open brackets, two *e* over *m* times capital *V* subscript two, close brackets
8 *u* equals a half sigma subscript upsilon squared all over *K*
9 sigma equals capital *M* small *y* small *c* all over capital *I*, plus capital *P* over capital *A*
10 gamma equals four *Q* over three pi *R* squared times, open brackets, *R* squared minus gamma squared, close brackets

D This is a typical simple calculation, and getting students to read it aloud provides practice in verbalizing formulae within the context of a complete sequence of calculation.

E The following formulae may be dictated to the class for the students to write down.

1 $\dfrac{V}{I}=R$

V over I equals R (all capital letters)

2 $P_1V_1=P_2V_2$

P subscript one V subscript one equals P subscript two V subscript two (all capital letters)

3 $\dfrac{1}{u}+\dfrac{1}{v}=\dfrac{1}{f}$

one over u plus one over v equals one over f (all small letters)

4 $F=\dfrac{mv^2}{r}$

capital F equals small m small v squared all over small r

5 $\dfrac{1}{R}=\dfrac{M}{EI}$

one over R equals M over EI (all capital letters)

6 $\dfrac{\sigma}{Yn}=\dfrac{M}{AhR_f}$

sigma over capital Y small n equals capital M over capital A small h capital R subscript small f

7 $A=2\pi R_c[R_c-\sqrt{(R_c^2-\dfrac{d^2}{4})}]$

capital A equals two pi capital R subscript small c, open square brackets capital R subscript small c minus square root open brackets capital R subscript small c squared minus small d squared over four, close brackets, close square brackets

8 $\tau=\dfrac{4Q}{3\pi R^4}(R^2-\gamma^2)$

tau equals four capital Q over three pi capital R to the power of four, open brackets, capital R squared minus gamma squared, close brackets

9 $F\propto\dfrac{M_1M_2}{R^2}$

F is proportional to M subscript one M subscript two all over R squared (all capital letters)

10 $\dfrac{T^2}{R^3}=\dfrac{4\pi^2}{GM}$

T squared over R cubed equals four pi squared over GM (all capital letters)

When the exercise has been completed, ask individual students to read out their answers, so that these can be written on the board. The class then approves or corrects individual students' versions.

24

unit 2
classwork
section 3

F Individual students are asked to read out the expressions 1 to 10. After each student, the rest of the class may be asked *Is that right?* and invited to correct the statement if the student's version was not correct.

exercises

exercise 1

1 AB is a *vertical straight* line of *length* 5 cm. AB is at *right angles* to BC, a *horizontal straight* line of *length* 8 cm.
2 DÊF is an *obtuse angle* of 113°.
3 GHI is a *right-angled* triangle having a *height* of 31 cm and a *length* of 54 cm.
4 JK̂L is an *acute angle* of 32°.
5 MNO is an *isosceles* triangle, having an angle NMO of 40°.
6 The lines PQ and RS *intersect* at X. The value of the *obtuse* angle is 105°.
7 The *vertical* line TU is *perpendicular* to the *horizontal* line VW.
8 The *straight* line yy¹ *bisects* the *obtuse* angle XYZ.

exercise 2

1	multiplication	6	multiply 34 by 7
2	multiplication	7	subtract x from x^2
3	addition	8	divide a^2b by c
4	division	9	add $3b$ to $2c$
5	subtraction	10	multiply a by b

exercise 3   The symbols and letters may be checked with reference to Parts **A** and **B** of Section 3.

drills

drill 1

1 What sort of angle is AB̂C?
It's an obtuse angle.
2 What sort of lines are GH and IJ?
They're parallel lines.
3 What sort of triangle is NOP?
It's an equilateral triangle.
4 What sort of angle is QR̂S?
It's a right angle.
5 What sort of lines are TU and VW?
They're intersecting lines.
6 What sort of angle is KL̂M?
It's an acute angle.
7 What sort of angle is XŶZ?
It's a reflex angle.
8 What sort of triangle is DEF?
It's an isosceles triangle.

drill 2

1 AB̂C
What sort of angle is AB̂C?
2 GH and IJ
What sort of lines are GH and IJ?
3 DEF
What sort of triangle is DEF?
4 QR̂S
What sort of angle is QR̂S?
5 NOP
What sort of triangle is NOP?
6 TU and VW
What sort of lines are TU and VW?
7 XŶZ
What sort of angle is XŶZ?
8 KL̂M
What sort of angle is KL̂M?

drill 3

1 *a squared plus b squared equals c*
2 *x to the power of a half over d equals thirty*
3 *a subscript two equals b minus c in brackets, all squared, all over a subscript one*
4 *seven point six times ten to the power of minus three, metres seconds to the power of minus one*
5 *x to the power of minus a half over a squared plus b squared equals one*
6 *open brackets, y over a minus x over b, close brackets, squared*

7 *cube root of, open brackets x squared plus y squared, close brackets, all over x*

8 *x squared over a squared plus y squared over b squared equals one*

drill 4

1 What's the square root of x?
twelve
2 What's y to the power of 4?
three point seven eight
3 What's *a* over *b*?
nine
4 What's x to the power of minus one?
forty
5 What's x to the power of minus seven?
ninety-one
6 What's y to the power of *n* minus one?
z
7 What's *d* to the power of one over four?
two point five
8 What's the cube root of *z*?
seven point two nine
9 What's *a* to the power of minus *n*?
nought point seven two one
10 What's y to the power of three over two?
seven hundred and twenty-one point five

drill 5

1 Is x equal to y?
No, x is greater than y.
2 Is *a* proportional to *b* squared?
No, a is equal to b squared.
3 Is *a* squared less than *b* squared?
No, a squared is equivalent to b squared.
4 Is theta ninety degrees?
No, theta is much less than ninety degrees.
5 Is *d* very small?
No, d tends to infinity.
6 Is gamma less than forty-five degrees?
No, gamma is greater than or equal to forty-five degrees.
7 Is z equal to fifty?
No, z is approximately equal to fifty.
8 Is *f* equal to *d* squared?
No, f is proportional to d squared.
9 Is alpha equal to beta?
No, alpha is not equal to beta.
10 Is y equal to fifty?
No, y is equal to plus or minus thirty.

unit 2
drills
drill 6

drill 6

1 What's pi *r* squared?
    pi r squared is the area of a circle.

2 What's pi *r* squared *h*?
    pi r squared h is the volume of a cylinder.

3 What's *bh*?
    bh is the area of a rectangle.

4 What's *h* cubed?
    h cubed is the volume of a cube.

5 What's *b* times *h* over two?
    b times h over two is the area of a triangle.

6 What's pi *d* one *d* two over four?
    pi d one d two over four is the area of an ellipse.

7 What's pi *r* squared *h* over three?
    pi r squared h over three is the volume of a cone.

activity

Give the following series of instructions to the students, who should carry them out. Students will need rulers, pencils and compasses.

When the instructions are complete and the students have finished constructing the drawing, they should compare their results. If there are any deviations from the drawing which should have been produced, the class should point out the mistakes.

Some of the words of instruction, which may be unfamiliar to the class, will need to be explained beforehand.

1   Draw a square of side 5 cm in the middle of the page. Label the square ABCD.
2   Draw two diagonal lines, AC and BD, in the square. Label the point of intersection X.
3   Draw a circle of radius 7 cm, with its centre at X.
4   Extend the diagonal AC to touch the circumference of the circle at A_1 and C_1.
5   Extend the diagonal BD to touch the circumference of the circle at B_1 and D_1.
6   Draw a line from A_1 to B_1 and from B_1 to C_1.
7   Measure the lengths of $A_1 B_1$ and $B_1 C_1$.
8   Measure the lengths of the diagonals AC and BD.
9   What sort of triangle is $A_1 B_1 C_1$?
10   Write down the values, from your drawing, of this formula: $A_1 B_1{}^2 + B_1 C_1{}^2 = A_1 C_1{}^2$

The activity may be continued by dividing the class into small groups, who each prepare a simple drawing together. The groups then work out a series of instructions for producing their drawings. One person from each group is appointed spokesman, and must relay these instructions to the other groups, who must follow them in order to produce similar drawings. When these are complete, they are compared to see how closely they correspond to the original drawing. This is repeated for each group. The drawings may be analysed to find out why mistakes have been made, and whether the instructions or the understanding of the instructions were at fault.

unit 3

classwork

SECTION 1   **describing position**

A *Students' books closed*. With the aid of suitable actions, objects (simple apparatus if available) and drawings, etc, present the following words of position:

above/over/on top of
under/underneath/below/beneath
behind/at the back of/in front of
between/in the middle of/in the centre of
near (to)/close to
by the side of/beside/on the right-hand/left-hand side
inside/outside/around
among/amongst

Some suggested methods of presenting/practising these words are:

1   Use various simple objects or pieces of apparatus in different positions relative to each other. For example,

teacher   *Where's the beaker?*
student   *It's above the bunsen burner, on top of the tripod.*

(If students are unfamiliar with these words, it may be best to take a small number at a time and practice these thoroughly.)

2   Get individual students to carry out simple instructions. For example, *Put the test-tube inside the beaker, Stand the beaker on top of the tripod*, and so on.

3   Get students in small groups or pairs to give each other similar simple instructions and carry them out.

When the words have been practised thoroughly, students should open their books and complete the statements as a class exercise. The descriptions may be completed in the following way. The different possible variants are given.

1   The cube is suspended *above/over* the small rectangular block.
The small rectangular block rests *on top of* the large rectangular block, *under/below/beneath/underneath* the cube.

2   The cone is *behind/at the back of* the rectangular block.
The sphere is *in front of* the rectangular block.

3   The cube is *between* the sphere and the cylinder.

4   The square is *in the middle/centre of* the circle.

5   The rectangular block is *near to/close to/on the right* (*-hand side*) *of/ by the side of/beside* the cube.
The cube is *near to/close to/on the left* (*-hand side*) *of/by the side of/ beside* the rectangular block.

6   There is water *inside* the beaker. The beaker stands *in/inside* a container of ice. There is ice *around* the beaker.

7   There is a sphere *among/amongst* the cubes.

8   The following words of spatial relation should be also introduced here:
These blocks are *touching* (each other).
These blocks are *separate/apart*.
These blocks are *joined*.
These two sides are *adjacent* (to each other).

B Students should use the table to make questions which they ask each other about the positions of objects such as those in the drawings. These drawings may be further exploited for building up written descriptions. As the description is built up orally, write the description on the board, either fully or in note form. The description can then be erased and students asked to write their own, or they can be asked to do so from the notes on the board.

C Descriptions will obviously vary, but suitable model versions might be:

1   A test-tube containing (=which contains) a small quantity of a liquid is held *over/above* a bunsen burner flame. It is held at an angle of about 45°. A piece of litmus paper is held *over* the open end of the test tube.
2   (i) A trough contains a quantity of water. A piece of phosphorus *on/in* a dish floats *on top of* the water. A bell-jar is placed *over* the phosphorus in the dish. There is a stopper *in the top of* the bell-jar.
    (ii) In this diagram, the level of the water *inside* the bell-jar is higher than the level *outside* the jar. The dish continues to float *on top of* the water.

D   Before students look at the exercise in their books, use a variety of objects to present the following words.

| inner | upper | front | inverted |
| outer | lower | rear | upturned |

The exercise can then be completed as follows:

1   outer container
2   inner container
3   upper block
4   lower block
5   rear end
6   front end
7   An inverted or upturned beaker.

E The description and diagram should be studied by the class together. Students then ask and answer questions about the parts of the apparatus listed. For example, *Whereabouts is the lid? It's on top of the apparatus.*

    As a further exercise, students can be asked to close their books, and reconstruct the description of the apparatus, either orally or both orally and then in written form.

F This may be carried out by students individually, or as a class exercise. The apparatus should resemble the drawing overleaf.

SECTION 2   **describing movement and action**

With *students' books closed*, use diagrams and actions, etc, to present the following words which express motion. (A simple working model made

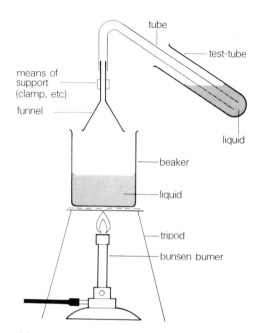

with a construction kit, or a piece of machinery or apparatus may be useful
for presenting many of these in a suitable context.)

pull	slide/slip
push	bend
raise/lift	tighten/loosen
lower	tilt
turn/rotate/twist/revolve	press
swing	oscillate

Present also *fall* and *rise*, which have more limited use grammatically,
due to their intransitivity. Conduct simple drills to practise these words. For
example, perform an action and ask *What am I doing?* Students reply.
Give students directions, individually and in groups. For example, *Lift up
your books*, etc. Get students in pairs telling each other to perform simple
actions. Use a simple model or device, to ask:
*What is it doing? What does the ... do when you ... ? What happens
when ... ?* and so on.

Ask simple questions which require words of motion to answer them.
For example,

How can I switch on the (tape recorder)?
Turn the knob to the right.
How can I open this jar?
Twist the top.
How can I make a telephone call?
Lift the receiver, and *turn* the dial.

Students open their books. The motions depicted in the drawings should
be identified, and students should write these down. The words are:

1	pull	8	swing	
2	push	9	slide	
3	lift/raise	10	(twist/turn) tighten/loosen	
4	lower	11	bend	
5	turn/rotate/revolve (used intransitively)	12	push/press	
6	twist	13	rise	
7	turn/rotate (used transitively)	14	fall	
		15	tilt	

B The class should study the diagram and the passage. The words *pulley, slope, string* and *attached to* may need to be explained. The expression *rests on* should be noted, as it occurs frequently in scientific description. The paragraph may then be completed by supplying the appropriate words of motion:

When the block slides down the slope, it *pulls* the string and *raises/lifts* the weight. At the same time, the pulley *revolves/turns/rotates* in a clockwise direction.

Attention is drawn to the present simple passive by illustrating the shift in emphasis between saying:

1 The block *pulls* the string.
2 The string *turns* the pulley.
3 The string *raises* the weight.

and:

4 The string *is pulled* by the block.
5 The pulley *is turned* by the string.
6 The weight *is raised* by the string.

C This may be covered as a class exercise to reinforce the use of the words of motion introduced so far, and give practice in the formation of the present simple passive tense. Note that *by means of* is frequently used instead of simply *by* in this type of description.

1 The belt turns the pulley.
  The pulley is turned by (means of) the belt.
2 The screwdriver tightens the screw.
  The screw is tightened by (means of) the screwdriver.
3 The ropes lower the block.
  The block is lowered by (means of) the ropes.
4 A 40 kN force bends the bar.
  The bar is bent by (means of) a 40 kN force.
5 The motor twists the wires.
  The wires are twisted by (means of) the motor.
6 The piston pushes the block.
  The block is pushed by (means of) the piston.
7 The spring pulls the block.
  The block is pulled by (means of) the spring.

D Both the present simple active and the present simple passive are used in this exercise. It is suggested that the exercise is completed by the students together in class with guidance from the teacher.

1   The correct key is pushed into the lock.
2   All the pins are raised, therefore the cylinder can be rotated/rotate.
3   When the cylinder is turned by the key, the lock opens.
4   When the lock is open, the key and the cylinder rotate back to their original position.
5   The key is pulled out of the lock.
6   When an incorrect key is used, the pins are not raised to the correct height.
7   The cylinder therefore cannot be rotated/rotate.

This exercise may be followed up by the class trying to reconstruct the description, looking at the diagrams only.

E This exercise may be done in class, to reinforce the use and formation of the present simple passive, and the use of words of position in the context of an experiment.

A small amount of white solid ammonium chloride *is placed in an evaporating dish*. A funnel *is inverted* over it. The dish *is heated* gently. A white vapour *is observed*. The white vapour *rises*. White crystals of ammonium chloride *form* on the inner surface of the funnel. No liquid stage *is observed*. It *is concluded* that ammonium chloride *changes* from a solid to a gas and from a gas to a solid directly, with no liquid stage.

After completing the passage, students may be asked to close their books and reconstruct the description of the experiment. They may also be asked to describe the apparatus from memory. For example,

The apparatus consists of an evaporating dish which contains solid ammonium chloride. There is an inverted funnel over the dish. There is a heat source below the dish.

SECTION 3   **describing direction**

A *Students' books closed*. By means of suitable diagrams, actions and examples, present and explain the meaning of the following words of direction. (The numbers correspond to the numbers in the drawings in the Student's Book.) Working models or pieces of simple machinery might help the presentation of some words.

1	up/upwards	9	into
2	down/downwards	10	through
3	sideways/to the left	11	out of
4	sideways/to the right	12	along
5	towards/forwards	13	up and down
6	backwards/away from	14	backwards and forwards/to and fro/from side to side
7	across		
8	round/around (clockwise/anti-clockwise)	15	in and out

Ask simple questions as a drill to practise these words. Use the question forms *Which way … ?* and *Which direction … ?* with any suitable model, apparatus or piece of equipment which is available. Get students to practise asking and answering similar questions.

Students should then open their books and be asked to identify the directions represented in the drawings.

B This description of an experiment may be completed as a class exercise.

A thistle funnel and a delivery tube are held *in* the *top* of a flask by means of a bung. Manganese oxide powder is in the *bottom* of the flask. Concentrated hydrochloric acid is poured *through* the thistle funnel until the end of the thistle funnel is just *below* the surface of the liquid.

The delivery tube passes *into* a trough of brine (salt and water). A gas-jar full of brine is *inverted* on *top* of a shelf, immediately *above* the end of the delivery tube.

The flask is held *over* a bunsen flame and the contents are heated. A reaction takes place in the flask, and a gas is produced. The gas passes *along* the delivery tube, *into* the jar of brine. Bubbles of gas rise *up through* the brine and the level of brine in the gas-jar goes *down*. The level of the brine *falls* until the jar is completely full of the gas.

C Words of direction, motion and position are used to complete the paragraphs describing the action of a rubber suction pad.

It will be useful if an actual suction pad can be used to demonstrate the action. Such pads are often used to hold hooks, soap dishes, etc, to walls in bathrooms and kitchens. They are concave, circular rubber pads, which, when pushed against a flat surface, will 'stick' to the surface due to the action of suction.

New words which are met in the passage should be explained as the exercise is completed. This may be treated as a class exercise, led by the teacher, which the students complete together.

The air pressure which acts *downwards* on the top of the pad is equal to the air pressure which acts *upwards between* the underneath of the pad and the lower surface.

When a force pushes the pad *downwards* (*towards* the surface), the air is expelled from underneath the pad. There is therefore a vacuum *between* the pad and the flat surface, and the air pressure pressing *downwards* on the pad is greater than the air pressure *underneath* the pad. The pad therefore 'sticks' to the surface.

When air enters *between* the pad and the flat surface, the air pressure *underneath* the pad rapidly becomes equal to the air pressure *above* the pad. When this happens, the pad no longer 'sticks' to the surface, and it returns to its original curved shape.

D This exercise may be completed in class, first orally, then by students writing in the correct words.

The weight W acts *downwards*, and this force is transmitted to the circumference of the spindle. This force *turns* the spindle and the toothed wheel in a *clockwise* direction. However, the wheel cannot *turn*

38

continuously because of the anchor. The ends of the anchor are alternately *raised* and *lowered* by the pendulum, as it *swings* from side to side. When the pendulum is vertical, the anchor allows the wheel to *turn*. When the pendulum is at the end of its swing, one end of the anchor is *lowered* and the wheel cannot *turn*. The time the pendulum takes to make one swing can be adjusted by moving the bob *up/upwards* or *down/downwards*.

The parts can be said to move in the following ways:

1 The weight   *downwards*
2 The spindle   *round/around*
3 The pendulum   *from side to side*
4 The ends of the anchor   *up and down*
5 The toothed wheel   *round/around*

E Having covered the previous part of the exercise thoroughly, students should now be familiar with the principle of a pendulum action. They should now be asked to describe this action themselves, using the outline notes. A suggested way of doing this is to have each part, 1 to 8, completed by a different student, with the teacher writing up exactly what is said. The class can then make any corrections together.

The completed description will read as follows:

1 The weight W acts downwards.
2 A force is transmitted to the circumference of the spindle.
3 This force turns the spindle and the toothed wheel in a clockwise direction.
4 However, the wheel cannot turn continuously because of the anchor.
5 This is raised and lowered by the pendulum which swings from side to side.
6 When the pendulum is vertical, the anchor allows the wheel to turn.
7 When the pendulum is at the end of its swing, one end of the anchor is lowered and the wheel cannot turn.
8 The time the pendulum takes to make one swing can be adjusted by moving the bob up or down.

Students may then be asked to explain how a pendulum works without the aid of notes, but with the diagram copied onto the board by the teacher.

F This may be completed as a class exercise.

Copper oxide *in* a porcelain boat is placed *inside* a large test-tube. Coal gas or hydrogen passes *into* the tube *through* the tube *on the left of* the diagram. The gas passes *over* the copper oxide. At the same time, the copper oxide is heated by a bunsen burner *below/underneath* the apparatus. The excess gas escapes *through* a small hole on the *upper* side of the test-tube, where it burns.

Again, students may be asked to close their books and describe the apparatus and the experiment from memory.

exercises

exercise 1

1   The diagram shows a simple cell.
2   The cell consists of a zinc container, a carbon rod, manganese dioxide inside a linen bag, and a gel of ammonium chloride.
3   The carbon rod is suspended in the centre of the container.
4   The carbon rod is surrounded by manganese dioxide inside the linen bag.
5   There is a space between the zinc container and the manganese dioxide.
6   The space is filled with ammonium chloride gel.
7   The carbon rod is suspended from the lid.
8   The lid covers the apparatus.

Students will need to have the use of *which* as a relative explained to them before attempting the second part of this exercise.

1   The diagram shows a simple cell, which consists of a zinc container, a carbon rod, manganese dioxide inside a linen bag, and a gel of ammonium chloride.
2   The carbon rod, which is suspended in the centre of the container, is surrounded by manganese dioxide inside the linen bag.
    or:
    The carbon rod, which is surrounded by manganese dioxide inside the linen bag, is suspended in the centre of the container.
3   There is a space between the zinc container and the manganese dioxide which is filled with ammonium chloride gel.
4   The carbon rod is suspended from the lid, which covers the apparatus.

exercise 2

1   The correct key is pushed into the lock. This raises the pins, and the cylinder can be rotated/rotate.
2   When the cylinder is rotated by the key, the lock opens.
3   The key and the cylinder then rotate back to their original position.
4   The key is pulled out of the lock.
5   When an incorrect key is used, the pins are not raised to the correct height, and the cylinder cannot be rotated/rotate.

exercise 3

The armature of the relay pivots around the knife-edge. When an electric current passes *through* the coil, the end of the armature A moves *towards* the core. The end of the armature B is therefore *raised*, and it pushes the *lower* contact spring, which *bends upwards* and touches the *upper* contact spring.

   When the electric current stops passing *through* the coil, the end of the armature A moves *away from* the core. The end B is *lowered*, and the contact spring *bends* back to its original position.

drills

drill 1

1 Where's the cone?
It's above the cube.

2 Which side of the cube is the sphere on?
It's on the right-hand side.

3 Is the hemisphere on the left-hand side of the cube?
Yes, it is.

4 Where's the pyramid?
It's in front of the cube.

5 Is the cylinder in front of the sphere?
No, it isn't, it's behind the sphere.

6 Is the cylinder behind the cube?
Yes, it is.

7 Which side of the sphere is the cube on?
It's on the left-hand side.

8 Is the cone underneath the cube?
No, it isn't, it's above the cube.

9 Is the cube behind the pyramid?
Yes, it is.

10 Is the cone on top of the cube?
No, it isn't, it's above the cube.

drill 2

1 What's on top of the cell?
A steel plate.

2 What's around the outside of the cell?
A steel casing.

3 What's between the steel plate and the steel casing?
An insulating gasket.

4 What's between the inner zinc cylinder and the outer steel casing at the bottom of the cell?
An insulator.

5 What's next to the zinc cylinder?
A potassium hydroxide electrolyte.

6 What's between the electrolyte and the outer steel casing?
Mercuric oxide.

7 Does the zinc cylinder touch the steel plate?
Yes, it does.

8 Does the zinc cylinder touch the steel casing?
No, it doesn't.

9 Is the potassium hydroxide electrolyte adjacent to the mercuric oxide?
Yes, it is.

10 Is the space inside the zinc cylinder empty?
Yes, it is.

drill 3

First twist the ends of the wires, and then slide the wires under the cord grip. Bend the wires, as shown, and then push the ends of the wires into the terminals. Finally, tighten the terminal and cord grip screws.

1 What do you do first?
   Twist the ends of the wires.
2 Then what do you do?
   Slide the wires under the cord grip.
3 What do you do next?
   Bend the wires, as shown.
4 What do you do after that?
   Push the ends of the wires into the terminals.
5 Finally what do you do?
   Tighten the terminal and cord grip screws.

drill 4

Water enters the tank at the bottom of the apparatus. When the level of the water rises, the cork is lifted. The lever turns around the axis of rotation, and the end of the lever with the mercury switch is lowered. When the lever is horizontal, mercury touches the two electrodes in the switch. When the level of the water falls, the lever turns about its axis and the mercury switch rises. Therefore the mercury does not touch the two electrodes in the switch, and there is no electrical contact.

The following is a key to the exercise—it is not spoken on the tape.

1 Where does water enter the tank?
   At the bottom.
2 What happens to the cork when the water level rises?
   The cork is lifted.
3 What does the lever move around?
   Around the axis of rotation.
4 What happens to the mercury switch as the cork rises?
   It is lowered.
5 What happens when the lever is horizontal?
   The mercury touches the two electrodes in the switch.
6 What happens when the level of the water falls?
   The lever turns around its axis.
7 What happens to the mercury switch as the water level falls?
   It rises.
8 What happens when the mercury switch rises?
   The mercury does not touch the two electrodes in the switch.

drill 5

1 A record is placed *on* the turntable, which *rotates* in a *clockwise* direction.
2 The pickup head is *lifted* and moved *towards* the record.

3   When the stylus is *over* the record, it is *lowered* until it touches the groove.

4   The stylus moves *across* the record as the record *turns*.

5   When the stylus is *at* the centre of the record, the pickup head is *lifted* and *moved away* from the centre of the turntable *to* its original position.

drill 6   This Drill is largely based on the account of the relay given in Exercise 3, which should be completed before the Drill is attempted.

1   Where is the armature pivoted?
Around the knife-edge.

2   When current is passed through the coil, what happens to the end of the armature A?
It moves towards the coil.

3   What happens at the same time to the end B?
It is raised.

4   What does the end B do as it is raised?
It pushes the lower contact spring upwards.

5   What happens to the lower contact spring?
It bends upwards towards the upper contact spring.

6   What happens when current stops passing through the coil?
The end of the armature A moves away from the coil.

7   What happens to the end B?
It is lowered.

8   What happens to the lower contact spring?
It bends back.

activity

The diagram is a simplified example of a moving-coil meter, such as may be used for measuring voltage or current in an electrical circuit.

It works on the principle that when current passes through the coil, a magnetic force is set up. Since the yoke is also a magnet, the attraction or repulsion between the two magnetic fields will cause the coil, and therefore the pointer, to turn. The degree to which these turn is dependent on the magnitude of the magnetic force in the coil, and hence on the magnitude of the current through the coil.

With guidance and prompting by the teacher, the class should be able to build up a description of the construction of this meter. Phrases such as *joined to, connected to, pivoted about* may be introduced to enable the construction of various elements to be described. It should be possible to describe the basic elements and their relation using language already encountered in this unit. For example: *the yoke is a hollow cylinder; the central core is a solid cylinder which has a coil wound around it; a pointer is attached to the upper axis of the core;* and so on.

The amount of new expressions introduced and the degree of detail of the description are left to the teacher's discretion.

unit 4

classwork

SECTION 1   **describing qualities of materials**

A *Students' books closed.* Present the class with a number of things made of different materials, and discuss their properties. Examples of the following materials would be useful:

paper	rubber	glass	steel
polythene	wood	wool	china

The properties can be elicited by question and answer: *What does rubber do?* (bending a piece of rubber) *It bends—it's pliable/flexible. Is glass flexible? How can we describe wool?* and so on. This should be continued until all the words describing properties which are listed in **A** have been introduced.

Students open their books. They should then be able to complete the statements describing properties.

Rubber is *flexible/pliable.*
Rubber is a *flexible/pliable* material.
Glass is *brittle/fragile.*
Glass is a *brittle/fragile* material.

Students should ask and answer questions using the list of materials and properties.

Illustrate how more than one property may be combined in a description—eg *steel is a strong rigid material*—and get students to make similar statements.

Discuss the properties of some other materials (have examples available) such as expanded polystyrene (a light plastic material used for insulation, packaging and disposable cups, etc), cellophane, fabric, etc.

B Illustrate how descriptions may be modified by:

extremely	quite
very	not very
fairly	

using either the examples in **A** or similar ones built up from the table. Get students to describe materials again, but this time using appropriate modifiers.

C This may be conducted as an oral class exercise, practising use of the modifiers in **B** and the contrast between opposite qualities. Students may subsequently be required to write down suitable answers to the questions formed from the notes, if desired.

D Either by using the diagrams, or by using suitable materials as examples, or by drawing on the board, etc, introduce the words:

ductile	conduct
malleable	conductor
	insulator

The statements should then be completed as follows (words which may need explanation are printed in bolder type):

A material which can be easily pulled out, or **stretched** into a long **wire** or **strand** is said to be *ductile*.

A material which can be easily **deformed** by **hammering** or **rolling** is said to be *malleable*.

When a substance allows heat or electricity to pass along it, it is said to *conduct* heat or electricity.

Copper (Cu) and aluminium (Al) are *conductors*, but glass and porcelain are *insulators*.

The table should be used as the basis for a brief oral exercise to drill these words, emphasizing the collocation between *good/poor* and *conductor/insulator*. The difference in the construction below should also be noted:

Copper is very ductile.

but:

Copper is **a** very ductile **material**.
Copper is **a** very good **conductor**.

E The regular forms of adjective comparison may be introduced here using the examples given in this section, or by means of the teacher's own presentation.

In the examples, the comparisons are modified by *slightly, much, a lot, considerably* and *far*.

The difference in the degree of contrast between these modifiers should be explained. For example, a scale such as the following may be used:

slightly
much/a lot
considerably
far

Explain that in forming the comparative, the *-er* form is generally used with monosyllabic adjectives, and that the combination *more* + adjective is used with words of more than one syllable. Introduce also the comparative *good, better*.

The exercise may be covered orally in class, but students may subsequently be required to write down their answers, either in class or for homework.

F Students will need to know the meanings of the words listed in this part. These may be explained with suitable examples before students look at this page in their books, or the words may be explained as this page is studied. The slight difference in formality between some of the words should be noted. For instance, *viscous* is a more formal scientific word than the more everyday *sticky*, although both may be found in science textbooks, etc. The words *powder, crystals*, etc, may be illustrated by examples such as:

soap powder/flakes
snowflakes
wood shavings
copper sulphate crystals
sugar granules

Iron filings are small particles of iron often used in magnetism experiments. Coarse and fine may also be applied to surface attributes—eg a *coarse/fine* cloth, or to objects, such as a *coarse/fine* brush.

The substances listed should be described as a class exercise. Students may then be asked to write their descriptions after suitable oral preparation.

SECTION 2   describing colours and appearances

A By means of objects of different colours, coloured pens, transparencies, etc, present the three primary colours of light and the range of colours in the spectrum. For example, ask: *What colour is this? What colour is the sky?* etc.

The spectrum and the primary colours of light are shown on the back cover of the Student's Book. The colours are as follows:

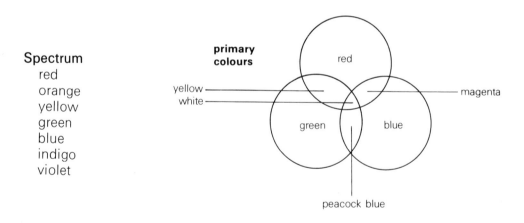

Spectrum
red
orange
yellow
green
blue
indigo
violet

Peacock blue is a widely accepted description of the colour formed by a mixture of blue and green light.

B By getting students to try to describe various things, point out that very often simple descriptions are not adequate to describe a given colour. It is necessary to introduce the concepts of **shades** of colour. (Examples in the room or from objects supplied can be given to illustrate things which are not precisely one colour.) The class should then practise describing the colours of various objects, using the shades given in the table.

C A common way of describing shade is to add the suffix *-ish* to a colour. This is set out here. The class should practise describing the shades of colour in this way. (For some colours, the suffix *-y* is sometimes used, as in *silvery, bluey,* etc.) Present also the use of noun modifiers of colour, for example *coffee brown, brick red, pea green, sky blue, pitch black,* etc.

The colours in the list should be identified, as they are often used in addition to those colours already introduced. Students should try to work out descriptions of these colours, using the methods of combining colour descriptions practised so far.

D Using suitable materials as examples explain the words *transparent* (*clear*), *opaque* and *translucent*. The statements in the Student's Book should then be completed as follows:

A material which allows light to pass through it is *transparent*.
Glass is *transparent*. (Glass is a *clear* substance.)
A material which does not allow light to pass through it is *opaque*.
Steel is *opaque*.
A material which allows some light to pass through it is *translucent*.
Ground glass or 'frosted' glass is *translucent*.
Substances which have no colour (like water) are *colourless*. Water is a *colourless* liquid. A white liquid is sometimes said to be *cloudy* or *milky*.
Carbon dioxide turns lime water *cloudy*.
When an object or substance is dirty, it is said to be *discoloured*.

E Using suitable objects, explain the words set out to describe **surface** or **appearance**.

The following materials may be useful as visual aids:

corrugated cardboard
a rough piece of wood
sandpaper
a battered piece of metal
a mirror
etc.

Suggested ways of completing the descriptions are as follows (some explanation of new words may be necessary):

1   Glass is a *transparent/clear* solid which usually has a *smooth shiny* surface.
2   Chalk is a porous solid which has a *rough powdery* surface.
3   Some cardboard is *corrugated* to give it extra strength.
4   The inside of a camera has a *matt black* surface.
5   Mercury is a liquid metal which has a *bright shiny silvery* appearance.
6   Sandpaper has a *rough abrasive* surface.
7   An unplaned piece of wood has a *coarse grainy* surface.
8   A piece of rubber has a *smooth matt* surface.

A brief oral exercise in describing appearance and texture should be carried out as a class exercise, using objects 1–5 as prompts.

F The table sets out a typical form of classification of the properties of metals. The teacher may begin the exercise by asking questions such as *What colour is aluminium? Is lead shiny? Which of the metals is magnetic?* and so on. Students then ask each other similar questions.

G Present three or more objects to the class. Students then produce a very brief description of each object under the headings of colour, appearance and texture. The objects should be chosen so that they can be described in terms of the vocabulary presented so far in this unit.

SECTION 3 describing a simple process and experiment

A The concepts of *hot, warm, cool* and *cold* should be introduced before students open their books. They are clearly relative terms, and may best be introduced with reference to, for instance, the weather in the students' country. (What is 'cool' on the equator may be 'warm' further north. Introduce the adjectives *high* and *low* which collocate with *temperature*. The terms *tepid* and *lukewarm* may be introduced, specifically with reference to liquids.

Students open their books and complete the statements:

2,000°C is very *high* temperature.
−50°C is a very *low* temperature.
1   hot   2   warm   3   cool   4   cold

The temperature applying to the weather may be discussed with reference to local conditions, so that the words *hot, warm, cool* and *cold* may be inserted as appropriate.

The water in this beaker is *lukewarm* (or *tepid*).

B Elicit from students, or if necessary introduce, the words needed to complete the table. This may be done with students' books closed, if desired, with reference to specific examples. For example: *This water is cold. What must be done to make it hot? It must be heated* and so on.

adjective	verb	noun
hot	heat	heat
warm	warm	warmth
cool	cool	coolness
cold	cool	cold/coldness

The concepts of *melt, freeze, boil, liquefy, solidify* and *vaporize* may either be introduced before the exercise, or while this is being conducted.

1   At normal temperatures, iron is a solid. However, when it is *heated* above 1,537°C, it *melts*.
2   Water is a liquid at normal temperatures. However, when it is *cooled* below 0°C, it *freezes*.
3   When water is *heated* to 100°C, it *boils*.

4   When a substance changes from a solid to a liquid, it is said to *liquefy*.
5   When a substance changes from a liquid to a solid, it is said to *solidify*.
6   When a substance changes from a liquid to a gas, it is said to *vaporize*.

C The regular formation of nouns and verbs from the adjectives given is as follows. Given the example, students should be able to complete the table themselves.

adjective	verb	noun
weak	weaken	weakness
tough	toughen	toughness
soft	soften	softness
hard	harden	hardness
rough	roughen	roughness
coarse	coarsen	coarseness

Non-regular verb and noun formation is dealt with in this table. The verbs and nouns should be elicited from the students, or introduced where necessary.

Where no verb exists (as with *resilient, flexible*, etc) the construction: *make something resilient/flexible*, etc may be used.

adjective	verb	noun
strong	strengthen	strength
resilient	make something resilient	resilience
brittle	embrittle	brittleness
flexible	make something flexible	flexibility
elastic	make something elastic	elasticity
pliable	make something pliable	pliability
smooth	smooth	smoothness
rigid	make something rigid	rigidity
ductile	make something ductile	ductility
malleable	make something malleable	malleability

D Using the adjective/verb/noun formation just covered, the exercise may be attempted by the class together, or by students individually.

Hardening. Medium and high carbon steel are not very *hard*, and so they must be *hardened*. They are *heated* slowly to a high temperature (above 700°C), and then rapidly *cooled* (or 'quenched'). Fully *hardened* steel is, however, extremely brittle and has poor shock resistance. The *brittleness* of *hardened* steel can be reduced and the quality of the metal increased by tempering. This process is described below.

Tempering. The metal is re-*heated* to a comparatively *low* temperature and again *quenched* at a carefully controlled temperature. The colour of the film of oxide on the brightened surface of the *hardened* steel gives a good approximate indication of the temperature of the steel. The oxide first turns a very pale yellow, and changes through a range of colours to dark blue as it is *heated*.

(Draw attention to the use of the words *increase* and *decrease* in this text, as they are used extensively in scientific writing.)

The table may be used as the basis for a class exercise, with students asking and answering questions about it. For example, *What colour is the oxide at 240°C? What's the temperature when the colour of the oxide is purple?* and so on.

E The diagram and description of the experiment should be studied as a class exercise in textual comprehension. A suggested approach is:

1   Students look at the diagram and read the passage to themselves.
2   Students ask the teacher about anything not understood.
3   Teacher reads the passage aloud while students follow.
4   Teacher asks the questions following the passage. Individual students answer.

(After question 8, which may be written by the teacher on the board as individual students give the stages of the experiment, the list of stages may be used as a prompt for students to reconstruct an account of the experiment. This may be followed up by written work, with students writing their own account using the notes only. This activity involves using the present simple passive construction.)

F Students have by now seen the expression ... *turns* (*red*) a number of times. A brief oral exercise on this construction may be carried out as follows. Present the construction in the context of the experiment just covered. For example, *The blue copper sulphate crystals turn white*. Ask students to use the construction to say what colour changes take place in the following situations. The answers are given in italics.

1   When red litmus paper is dipped into an alkali (eg sodium hydroxide, NaOH).
    The red litmus paper turns blue.
2   When blue litmus paper is dipped into an acid (eg sulphuric acid H_2SO_4).
    The blue litmus paper turns red.
3   When a piece of white porcelain is held in a candle flame.
    The white porcelain turns black. (It becomes coated with carbon).
4   When carbon dioxide is passed through lime water.
    The lime water turns cloudy or milky. (A simple test for carbon dioxide).
5   When water is added to cold dry white copper sulphate crystals.
    The crystals turn blue.

exercises

exercises 1
1 Steel with a high carbon content is less ductile than steel with a low carbon content.
2 Dead mild steel is softer than mild steel.
3 Medium carbon steel is harder than mild steel.
4 High carbon steel is less ductile than dead mild steel and mild steel.
5 Medium carbon steel is less ductile than mild steel.
6 Medium carbon steel is less hard than high carbon steel.
7 Mild steel is harder than dead mild steel.
8 High carbon steel is much harder than dead mild steel.
9 Dead mild steel is far softer than high carbon steel.
10 Mild steel is considerably more ductile than high carbon steel.

exercise 2   Suitable answers are:
1 Silver is a shiny white solid.
2 Water is a colourless liquid.
3 Copper is a reddish-brown solid.
4 Iron is a greyish-white solid.
5 Coffee is a brownish liquid.
6 Glass is a transparent solid.
7 Sulphur is a pale yellow solid.
8 Milk is a white liquid.
9 Sulphuric acid is a colourless liquid.
10 Coal is a black solid.
11 Sand is a yellowish brown powder.
12 Sugar is a fine white (or brown) crystalline solid.

exercise 3
1 When aluminium is heated to 659·70°C, it melts.
2 When water is cooled to 0°C, it freezes.
3 When steel is hardened, it becomes brittle.
4 When hardened steel is heated to 270°C it turns purple.
5 When water is heated above 100°C, it vaporizes.
6 When ice is heated to 0°C, it melts.
7 When liquid steel is cooled, it solidifies.
8 When rubber is vulcanized, it becomes tougher.
9 When copper is heated, it becomes more ductile.
10 When glass is toughened, it becomes more resilient.
11 When blue copper sulphate crystals are heated, they turn white.
12 When steel is heated to 300°C, the film of oxide turns dark blue.

drills

drill 1

1 What about strength?
Aluminium is less strong than copper.

2 What about resistance?
Aluminium has a higher resistance than copper.

3 What about weight?
Aluminium is lighter than copper.

4 What about cost?
Aluminium is cheaper than copper.

5 What about corrosion resistance?
Aluminium has a higher corrosion resistance than copper.

6 What about conductivity?
Aluminium is a poorer conductor than copper.

7 What about ease of soldering?
Aluminium is less easy to solder than copper.

drill 2

1 Is copper a better conductor than lead?
Yes, it's far better.

2 Is brass a better conductor than copper?
No, it's much poorer.

3 Is aluminium a better conductor than lead?
Yes, it's much better.

4 Is brass a better conductor than zinc?
Yes, it's slightly better.

5 Is lead a poorer conductor than zinc?
Yes, it's slightly poorer.

6 Is copper a poorer conductor than lead?
No, it's far better.

7 Is zinc a better conductor than copper?
No, it's much poorer.

8 Is zinc a poorer conductor than lead?
No, it's slightly better.

drill 3

1 Copper's brown, isn't it?
No, it's not; it's a reddish colour.

2 Gold's a dull white, isn't it?
No, it's not; it's a bright yellow colour.

3 Mercury's a sort of greyish colour, isn't it?
No, it's not; it's a silvery-white colour.

4 Sulphur's pale green, isn't it?
No, it's not; it's a pale yellow colour.

5 Lead's a silvery colour, isn't it?
No, it's not; it's a bluish-white colour.

6 Tin's grey, isn't it?
No, it's not; it's a silvery-white colour.

7 Silver's a bright yellow colour, isn't it?
No, it's not; it's a bright white colour.

8 Magnesium's a dull greyish colour, isn't it?
No, it's not; it's a silvery-white colour.

9 Zinc's brown, isn't it?
No, it's not; it's a bluish-white colour.

10 Aluminium's a goldish colour, isn't it?
No, it's not; it's a light white colour.

drill 4

1 Glass is opaque.
No it isn't, it's transparent.

2 Silver is dull.
No it isn't, it's shiny.

3 Water is coloured.
No it isn't, it's colourless.

4 Glass is rough.
No it isn't, it's smooth.

5 Aluminium is heavy.
No it isn't, it's light.

6 Lead is transparent.
No it isn't, it's opaque.

7 Polythene is brittle.
No it isn't, it's resilient.

8 Steel is weak.
No it isn't, it's strong.

9 Ice is hot.
No it isn't, it's cold.

10 Steel is flexible.
No it isn't, it's rigid.

drill 5

1 What's done to water to make it hot?
It's heated.

2 What's done to steel to make it hard?
It's hardened.

3 What's done to a metal to make it cold?
It's cooled.

4 What's done to an object to make it clean?
It's cleaned.

5 What's done to paper to make it strong?
It's strengthened.

6 What's done to glass to make it tough?
It's toughened.

7   What's done to wood to make it smooth?
It's smoothed.

8   What's done to water to make it turn into ice?
It's frozen.

drill 6

1   What does heating do to the metal?
Heating increases its ductility.

2   What does hardening do to the metal?
Hardening reduces its toughness.

3   What does strengthening do to the metal?
Strengthening increases its resilience.

4   What does hardening do to the metal?
Hardening reduces its flexibility.

5   What does toughening do to the metal?
Toughening reduces its weakness.

6   What does tempering do to the metal?
Tempering increases its strength.

7   What does cooling do to the metal?
Cooling increases its hardness.

8   What does polishing do to the metal?
Polishing increases its smoothness.

9   What does heating do to the metal?
Heating increases its malleability.

10   What does cooling do to the metal?
Cooling reduces its softness.

activity

Present the class with a number of different substances, which should be examined and discussed in turn. Draw up as complete a description as possible for each of them, eliciting and presenting vocabulary as necessary. This activity will probably involve the presentation of much new vocabulary in order to be able to describe the qualities of the substances, but this vocabulary will be clearly contextualized around the objects and substances presented. For example, if oil is presented, a description may involve expressions such as *thick, sticky, viscous*, etc. Some suitable materials which are easily available for presentation are:

porcelain	oil
perspex	sand
cellophane	polythene
water	expanded polystyrene (very light, often used in packing)
soap	cream
toothpaste	

A further development of this activity may be conducted in the following ways. Ask every student to choose a material, either from a list supplied or on his own. The student must then write as full a description of this material as possible. Each student then reads out his description, without revealing what the material is. The rest of the class must discover, from the description, the identity of the material.

unit 5

classwork

SECTION 1   classification, definition and description

A With *students' books closed*, present three lists of substances on the board, without stating how these are grouped. Try to elicit from students that they are divided into *elements*, *compounds* and *mixtures*. Students may not know these words in English, in which case the teacher should supply the words if the students are thinking along the right lines. Students may suggest other distinctions during this activity—eg that the substances are solids, liquids or gases. (In this case, point out that this is not the way they are grouped here, although it is possible to group them in this way.)

Students should try to explain the meanings of the words *element*, *compound* and *mixture*. *Elements* are substances which cannot be broken down further into other constituent substances. *Compounds* are chemical combinations of elements which cannot be separated by normal physical means. *Mixtures* are substances which exist together but are not chemically combined. Any of the three may exist as either solids, liquids or gases. Suitable lists of elements, compounds and mixtures are:

elements	compounds	mixtures
carbon	water	air
oxygen	carbon dioxide	sand and water
sulphur	chalk	
hydrogen	common salt	
iron	hydrogen peroxide	

Students should then open their books, and complete the statements as follows:

The basic constituents of all matter are *elements*. Some of these exist freely in nature (carbon, iron, copper, etc). (*Exist freely* means that they occur naturally in their pure form.) When two or more *elements* are chemically joined together, they form a *compound*. When two or more *elements* or *compounds* are mixed together but not chemically combined, they form a *mixture*. *Elements*, *compounds* and *mixtures* can be either solids, liquids or gases.

 B Discuss how the diagram can be completed to show the classification of matter into solids, liquids, gases and compounds, mixtures and elements. Either as a class exercise or individually, students should complete the diagram as shown opposite.
Examples are given in the Student's Book of simple statements which express general truth. The terms *states*, *classes* and *forms* are introduced. The students should be aware that statements of general truth such as these are made using the present simple tense. Two examples of definitions are given. Definitions generally employ the present simple tense, and are worded in a standard way along the pattern:

A molecule is defined as ...
An atom is defined as ...

C A simple description of an atom is given in the Student's Book. This statement, the diagram, and the statements about the atom on the next

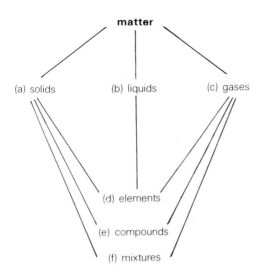

matter
(a) solids   (b) liquids   (c) gases

(d) elements

(e) compounds

(f) mixtures

page should be studied by the class. Any unfamiliar terms in these statements should be explained. (*Gain*, *lose*, *become* may need to be presented.) When these examples have been studied and understood, students go on to make their own statements about the atom, using the notes. Some distinction between the use of the definite and indefinite article may need to be introduced here. *An atom* is used in 1 because it refers to any atom. Further statements refer to *the nucleus* and *the proton*, etc, because these have already been identified in 1 and 2.

1 An atom consists of a nucleus and electrons.
2 The nucleus consists of protons and neutrons.
3 The proton has a positive charge.
4 The proton has a mass of $1 \cdot 672 \times 10^{-27}$ kg.
5 The neutron has no electrical charge.
6 The mass of the proton is equal to the mass of the neutron.
7 The electron has a negative electrical charge and negligible mass.
8 When the number of electrons is equal to the number of protons, the atom is neutral.
9 When an atom gains an electron, it becomes a negative ion.
10 When an atom loses an electron, it becomes a positive ion.
11 The atomic weight of an atom is equal to the number of protons plus the number of neutrons.
12 The atomic number of an atom is equal to the number of protons in the atom.

D The passage on radioactivity should be studied, and new words explained. The language may be more advanced than that met so far, but the principle explained should be fairly readily understandable. The emphasis should be placed upon general comprehension of the passage rather than a complete grasp of all the constructions and expressions. Some of the new words may be presented before the passage is studied, if desired.

The questions following the passage should then be answered with full statements, giving students practice in making formal descriptive statements. These answers may be prepared orally and then written up on the board by the teacher or by the students individually. In either case, the end product of the exercise should be a series of written statements about radioactivity.

1   Certain heavy elements (eg uranium) emit high energy radiation.
2   This radiation consists of alpha-, beta- and gamma-rays.
3   This radiation can be shown to exist by its behaviour in a magnetic field.
4   Alpha-rays consist of alpha particles.
5   Alpha particles are helium atoms which have lost two electrons.
6   Beta-rays consist of beta particles, which are fast-moving electrons.
7   Gamma-rays have a very short wavelength and high penetrating power.
8   The rays can be detected by photographic means.
9   Alpha particles have a positive charge.
10 Beta particles have a negative charge.

SECTION 2   describing and predicting

A *Students' books closed.* If possible, two bar magnets or compasses should be used in this presentation, to demonstrate the phenomenon of magnetism. When a bar magnet is freely suspended about its centre, it will orientate itself along a north–south axis. When two magnetic poles are brought close together, like poles are found to repel, unlike poles to attract. This demonstration will involve the presentation of *attract* and *repel* and should include an introduction to predictive statements of the conditional (1) type. For example,

What will happen if I bring two north poles together?

and:

If a bar magnet is suspended about its centre, it will turn to point north–south.

Try to elicit from students a generalized statement of the form: *Like poles repel, unlike poles attract.*

 Students open their books. The phenomena demonstrated above are described in the Student's Book. The description should be studied, and new words explained. Ask general comprehension questions about the material presented in this description, involving the *if . . . will . . .* construction as much as possible.

From the description, a statement is made summarizing the phenomenon. This is in the form of a statement of general truth. Use the table to make simple predictive statements based on the summary of magnetism.

B This part introduces the terms: *expand/expansion, contract/contraction.* These words may be presented before students look at this part in their books, or with the relevant page in front of them. They should complete the description as follows:

If a metal bar is heated, its dimensions will *increase.* When substances *increase* their dimensions (volume, area or length) when they are heated, they are said to *expand.* This phenomenon is known as *expansion.* When a substance decreases in length, area or volume, it is said to *contract.* This phenomenon is known as *contraction.*

Students make simple predictive statements from the table. (If the substances are heated, they will expand. If they are cooled, they will contract.)

C Presentation of predictive statements is continued in the context of tensile and compressive forces. If the terms *stretch* and *squash* (or *squeeze*) are introduced before looking at this part, the description may then be completed as a class exercise, with the teacher asking comprehension questions during and after the activity.

A material is said to be in tension when the forces applied to it tend to *stretch* the material. For example, if a mass is hung on the end of a length of rubber, the rubber will be in tension. A force which *produces* tension is known as a tensile force. A tensile force will *increase* the length of the material on which it acts.
A material is said to be in compression when the forces applied to it tend to *squash* or *squeeze* the material. For example, if a rubber eraser is *squeezed* between the fingers, the rubber will be in compression. A force which *produces* compression is known as a compressive force. A compressive force will *reduce* the length of the material on which it acts.
If a force is applied to a metal wire which is *suspended* vertically, the wire will *increase* in length, according to the magnitude of the force. The wire is then said to *extend,* and the increase in length is said to be the *extension.*

D The passage and the diagrams are studied by the class, the teacher reading and explaining new terms. The complete passage illustrates a sequence of predictive statements leading to a statement of general truth in the form of a law. The teacher may ask simple comprehension questions throughout the passage in order to establish and check comprehension. After studying the passage, students may be asked to reconstruct an account of the experiment, orally and/or in writing.
The notes in this exercise are used to form correct predictive statements about the experimental situation.

1   If masses are added to the wire, the force in the wire will increase.
2   If a load is applied to the wire, the wire will be extended.
3   If a vernier scale is used, the measurement of length will be more accurate.
4   If the stress is less than the elastic limit, the wire will return to its original length.

5 If the elastic limit is not exceeded, stress will be proportional to strain.
6 If a graph of stress against strain is plotted, it will be found to be a
   straight line.
7 If the load is too great, the elastic limit will be exceeded.
8 If the load is too great, stress will not be proportional to strain.

SECTION 3 detailed description

A If desired, the process of including several descriptive elements to form
a single noun group as in *a large diameter cylindrical steel tube* may be
introduced before work on this part is begun. Alternatively, the exercise in
the Student's Book may be treated as a class exercise to introduce the
building up of noun groups. It is difficult to give firm rules for pre-
modification, but a useful guide in these exercises is that the word order
often follows the pattern:

	size	shape	colour	material	noun
as in:	*a large*	*circular*	*black*	*plastic*	*plate*

The statements should be completed as follows:

1 The internal diameter of a tube is sometimes called the *bore*. The
   diameter of this tube is the same all along its length. It is therefore said
   to be *uniform*, and we can say: The tube has a *uniform bore*.
   We can also say: It's a *uniform-bore* tube.
2 This plug has three *pins*. We can therefore say: It's a *three-pin* plug.
   It can carry a current of 13 amps, so we can say: It's a *thirteen-amp
   three-pin* plug.
3 This container is cylindrical. It is made of metal. We can therefore say:
   It's a *cylindrical metal* container.
   This tube has a large diameter. It's made of steel. We can therefore
   say: It's a *large-diameter steel* tube.
1 A mercury thermometer.
2 A rectangular steel bar.
3 A small-bore glass tube.
4 A three-speed electric motor.
5 A twelve-inch black plastic disc.

   The teacher may wish to introduce further examples of noun-group
formation of a similar kind.

B This may be treated as a class exercise in description. The following
words are important in the exercise:

   as: to indicate simultaneous action
   since: as a connective (to replace *therefore*)

1 A laboratory thermometer consists of a sealed glass tube with a bulb at
   one end.
2 The tube has a small, uniform bore, and air is removed from it.

3   The bulb contains mercury or alcohol, which can pass along the tube.

4   As the temperature increases, the mercury or alcohol expands.

5   As the liquid expands, it travels along the tube.

6   Since the tube has a uniform bore, distances measured along the tube are proportional to changes in temperature.

7   Since the side of the tube is marked with a scale, the temperature can be read directly from the position of the mercury or alcohol.

8   Since the liquid expands a certain amount for a unit rise in temperature, the liquid will travel further along a small-bore tube for a given rise in temperature.

The construction:

   The smaller the bore, the longer the thermometer.
   The larger the bore, the shorter the thermometer.

is explained with reference to the principle of the thermometer. The following is a class exercise in this construction.

C

1   When a metal is compressed, the larger the force the greater the compression.

2   When a metal is heated, the higher the temperature the more ductile the material.

3   When two magnets are brought together, the nearer the poles the greater the force.

4   When a force is applied to a wire, the larger the force the greater the extension.

5   When a current is passed through a wire, the higher the current the greater the heating effect.

6   When a gas is compressed, the higher the pressure the smaller the volume.

7   When a thermometer is heated, the higher the temperature the longer the column of mercury.

8   When steel is made, the higher the carbon content the harder the steel.

exercises

exercise 1

1 Matter exists in three states.
2 All matter can be divided into compounds, mixtures and elements.
3 All matter is made up of atoms and molecules.
4 An atom consists of a nucleus and one or more electrons.
5 The electrons revolve round the nucleus of the atom.
6 The nucleus consists of neutrons and protons.
7 Protons have a positive charge.
8 Neutrons do not have an electrical charge.
9 The atomic weight of an element is equal to the number of protons plus the number of neutrons in the nucleus of an atom of the element.
10 The radiation emitted by certain heavy elements consists of three types of ray.

exercise 2

1 If a block of ice is heated above 0°C, it will melt.
2 If oxygen is cooled to −182·97°C, it will **liquefy**.
3 If a tensile force is applied to a metal wire, its length will increase.
4 If a rectangular metal block is heated, its volume will increase.
5 If the north pole of a magnet is brought near the south pole of another magnet, the poles will attract each other.
6 If the south pole of a magnet is brought near the south pole of another magnet, the poles will repel each other.
7 If the end of a copper bar is heated, heat will travel along the bar.
8 If an electric current is passed along a conductor, the conductor will become hot.

exercise 3

1 Since mercury freezes at about −39°C, a mercury thermometer cannot be used below this temperature.
2 Since temperatures in laboratory work are often higher than 78°C, an alcohol thermometer cannot be used for this work.
3 Since a mercury thermometer can be used between −39°C and 357°C, it can be used for laboratory work.
4 Since room temperature is normally less than 78°C, alcohol thermometers can be used for measuring room temperature.
5 Since alcohol is fairly cheap, alcohol thermometers are used more than mercury thermometers to measure room temperature.

drills

drill 1

1 Is carbon a mixture?
   No, carbon's an element.
2 Are protons neutral?
   No, protons are positive.
3 Is water an element?
   No, water's a compound.
4 Are electrons positive?
   No, electrons are negative.
5 Is helium a compound?
   No, helium's an element.
6 Is glass an element?
   No, glass is a compound.
7 Is sulphur a gas?
   No, sulphur's a solid.
8 Are neutrons charged?
   No, neutrons are neutral.

drill 2

1 What do atoms consist of?
   Atoms consist of electrons, protons and neutrons.
2 What does steel consist of?
   Steel consists of iron and carbon.
3 What does water consist of?
   Water consists of hydrogen and oxygen.
4 What does alpha-radiation consist of?
   Alpha-radiation consists of alpha particles.
5 What does beta-radiation consist of?
   Beta-radiation consists of fast-moving electrons.
6 What does white light consist of?
   White light consists of all the colours of the spectrum.
7 What do molecules consist of?
   Molecules consist of numbers of atoms.
8 What do compounds consist of?
   Compounds consist of two or more elements.

drill 3

1 What will happen to water if it is cooled below 0°C?
   It will freeze.
2 What will happen to a steel bar if it is heated?
   It will expand.
3 What will happen to ice if it is heated to 0°C?
   It will melt.
4 What will happen if a tensile force is applied to a steel wire?
   It will extend.

5 What will happen to alcohol if it is cooled?
It will contract.

6 What will happen if two north poles are brought near to each other?
They will repel.

7 What will happen to oxygen if it is cooled to $-182 \cdot 97°C$?
It will boil.

8 What will happen if oxygen and hydrogen are combined chemically?
They will form water.

drill 4

1 Will steel expand if it's heated?
Yes, it will.

2 Will steel wire increase in length if it's compressed?
No, it won't, it will decrease.

3 Will like magnetic poles attract?
No, they won't, they'll repel.

4 Will water boil if it's cooled to 0°C?
No, it won't, it'll freeze.

5 Will a metal wire extend if it's stretched?
Yes, it will.

6 Will unlike magnetic poles attract?
Yes, they will.

7 Will water contract if it's heated?
No, it won't, it'll expand.

8 If the elastic limit of a material is not exceeded, will stress be proportional to strain?
Yes, it will.

drill 5

1 Does the tube have a uniform bore?
Yes, it's a uniform-bore tube.

2 Does the plug have three pins?
Yes, it's a three-pin plug.

3 Does the thermometer have mercury inside it?
Yes, it's a mercury thermometer.

4 Does the steel have a high carbon content?
Yes, it's a high-carbon steel.

5 Is the magnet a rectangular bar shape?
Yes, it's a rectangular bar magnet.

6 Is the container a cylinder made of metal?
Yes, it's a cylindrical metal container.

7 Does the motor have three speeds?
Yes, it's a three-speed motor.

8 Does the switch have three positions?
Yes, it's a three-position switch.

9   Does the cell contain nickel and cadmium?
Yes, it's a nickel-cadmium cell.

10   Is it a thermometer containing alcohol for measuring room temperature?
Yes, it's an alcohol room thermometer.

drill 6

1   If the temperature of the metal bar is high, will the expansion be great?
Yes, the higher the temperature the greater the expansion.

2   If a large force is applied to the wire, will the extension be large?
Yes, the larger the force the larger the extension.

3   If the magnetic force is large, will there be a strong attraction?
Yes, the larger the magnetic force the stronger the attraction.

4   If the magnetic poles are brought near to each other, will the force be great?
Yes, the nearer the magnetic poles the greater the force.

5   If a gas is placed under high pressure, will the volume become smaller?
Yes, the higher the pressure the smaller the volume.

6   If the current in a wire is high, will there be a large heating effect?
Yes, the higher the current the larger the heating effect.

7   If there is a high carbon content in the steel, will the steel be hard?
Yes, the higher the carbon content the harder the steel.

8   If the temperature is high, will the metal become ductile?
Yes, the higher the temperature the more ductile the metal.

9   If the temperature is low, will the column of mercury be short?
Yes, the lower the temperature the shorter the column of mercury.

10   If the bore is narrow, will the thermometer be long?
Yes, the narrower the bore, the longer the thermometer.

activity

This takes the form of an exercise in classifying different types of matter, and should involve students in deciding how materials may be classed, and how solid matter may be further sub-divided.

The division of matter into solids, liquids and gases should be taken as the starting point. Ask students to suggest how solid matter may be further subdivided. Ask them to suggest as many different forms of solid matter as they can think of. The list can then be examined to see if the substances can be grouped into categories. It should be possible to divide them broadly into **metals**, **plastics** and **ceramics**, and **organic materials** such as wood, wool, etc. (Ceramics are materials such as china, glass, porcelain, etc.) Metals may be further sub-divided into **ferrous metals** (containing some proportion of iron) and **non-ferrous** metals (cast iron, steel.) Plastics may be sub-divided into thermoplastics (PVC, polythene, celluloid, nylon, polystyrene), and thermosetting plastics (bakelite, epoxy resins).

Having drawn up the sub-categories and placed the appropriate materials within them, the scheme should then be examined to see if lists of materials in the various categories can be extended. When the scheme is felt to be fairly complete, students may be asked to make statements describing the classification of materials.

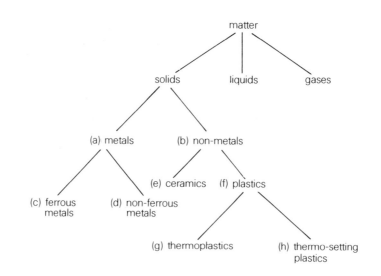

unit 6

classwork

SECTION 1 **simple instructions**

A Students give each other instructions using the table with *open*, *close* and *shut*. These instructions should be carried out correctly by the student receiving them. The teacher may ask students to give further instructions, using objects available in the classroom.

Imperatives with a limited number of verbs with prepositions are then introduced and practised in the same way, using the second table. (It can be pointed out that it is possible to transpose the preposition, for example: *Pick your book up/Pick up your book*. Students then make up their own instructions using the verbs with prepositions given. The exercise may be repeated with the prepositions transposed wherever possible.

B Words of instruction frequently used in the context of science are introduced.

Place is often used rather than *put* as an instruction. For example; *Place some copper sulphate crystals on a filter paper*.

The words which correspond to the illustrations should be introduced in the context of actions performed by the teacher. Students should then be asked to complete the instructions for the actions shown in the drawings.

1 *Pour* some water into a beaker.
or:
Fill a beaker with water.
2 *Insert* a tube into a test-tube.
3 *Remove/withdraw* the stopper from the container.
4 *Connect/Attach/Fix* the wire to the terminal.
5 *Measure* the length of the rod.
6 *Calculate/Find* the result of the equation.
7 *Draw/sketch* a diagram of the apparatus.
8 *Observe* the reaction which takes place.

C The flow chart may be used for a series of activities:
1 Students use it to give instructions for opening a door. Words indicating sequence may be introduced here. For example: *first, next, then, after that, finally*. The two alternative paths through the chart should prompt the expressions *If the key turns, open the door* and *If the key doesn't turn, remove the key from the lock*.
2 Introduce the expression of instruction using *should*. The chart can then be used to prompt expressions such as:
    What should I do first?
    First you should ...
The present perfect may be introduced here, as in the pattern:
    When you have ..., you should ...
3 The passive form, as it is often used to express instruction in an indirect form, is demonstrated in the paragraph. This form of instruction should be noted here, as it is developed further in the next section. Having studied this paragraph in class, students may be asked to construct a similar paragraph using the passive voice, with only the flow chart as a prompt.

D As a follow-up class activity, the teacher and students together may try constructing a flow chart for a simple series of operations. For example, operating a radio set, taking a photograph, etc. This can be done by first eliciting a series of instructions, and then building these into a suitable flow chart.

SECTION 2   instruction and explanation

A The diagram of a simple cell should be studied in class and any new words explained. The diagram should be familiar to students of general science. (H_2SO_4 is the chemical symbol for sulphuric acid.) Students should complete the instructions, either as a class exercise, or by students first working individually and then discussing answers with the whole class.

1   Fill
2   Arrange
3   Connect
4   Note
5   Wait
6   Observe

   The teacher should guide the class in their completion of numbers 7 to 12, since some of the words required may be new. If possible, the action to be described should be presented to the class in order to present or elicit the appropriate instruction.

7   Remove
8   Disconnect
9   Replace
10   Re-connect
11   Read
12   Compare

Point out the use of the prefixes *dis-* and *re-* as in *disconnect* and *re-connect*.

B This paragraph is in effect a series of instructions, but these are in the indirect form of passive sentences. The class should attempt to re-write instructions 7 to 12 in the same way, using the notes supplied, in order to construct a complete paragraph. For example,

   The electrodes should be removed from the container and the wires disconnected. The copper and zinc electrodes should be replaced with carbon and zinc electrodes. The galvanometer should then be reconnected and the value of the deflection should be noted. The value of the deflection should then be compared with the value for copper and zinc.

C This paragraph is studied in a similar way, and from the information a sequence of instructions is evolved for repeating the experiment. Each

instruction should begin with a word of direct instruction. Model answers
are:

1 Repeat the experiment using copper and zinc electrodes.
2 Weigh the electrodes before and after the experiment.
3 Allow the cell to function for some time before the electrodes are
   weighed for the second time.
4 Compare the weights of the electrodes before and after the experiment.
5 Consider the results carefully.
6 Try to deduce what has happened in the cell during the course of the
   experiment.

D The diagrams and passage should be studied carefully in class, new
words being explained and comprehension questions being asked
throughout. The passage may be studied quite slowly, ensuring that
students understand not only the language but also the principle of
operation of a cell.

More connecting words are introduced in this passage, and their
function in the language should be made clear. They are: *it follows that, as
a result, therefore.*

When the passage has been thoroughly covered and understood,
students cover up the text, and the class is asked to explain the action of
the cell using the sequence of diagrams only. Students should attempt to
make use of the above connectives in their accounts.

This explanation may be written up in note form by the teacher, and if
desired, individual students can then be asked to explain short sections of
the process using the notes and diagrams. Further possible exploitations of
this exercise include asking students to write an account of the process,
using only the diagrams, or the diagrams and the notes made by the class.
Individual students may be asked to attempt to explain the process orally,
using only the diagrams. (A note to the student is given in **E**.)

SECTION 3   **description of a process**

A The diagram represents the sequences in the process by which electric
power is generated. (The word *grid* in the sense in which it is used here
refers to the grid system by which electricity is distributed to users, as for
instance in the United Kingdom.) The passage may be read out or played
to the students, or they should be told to read it to themselves. Ask
questions on the text to establish students understand it fully. They should
then be able to reproduce an account of the generation of electricity using
only the notes in 1–5.

The notes should be used in conjunction with the diagram alone. It
would therefore be useful if this could be re-drawn on the blackboard or
an overhead projection transparency could be used.

Students reproducing the sequence of events should make use of
connecting words of sequential relation such as *first, next, then,* etc.

B The sequence of stages is reduced to a shorter set of notes. Students should put this representation of the sequence into a complete account of the process, as an oral exercise.

C The word *transformation* should be introduced in the context of *a transformation of energy*. The sequence of energy transformation is set out in the block diagram. (In fact, the transformations could be traced back further to the sun's energy creating plant life, which turns to fossil fuel). Students should be asked to give an account of these transformations, using the expressions: ... is *transformed into/is turned into/becomes* ...

Students then complete the 3 sentences describing the process. The words to be inserted into the description are: *generate, produce, produces, transformed*.

D The flow chart may then be used as a basis for further description of sequence. Ask students to describe what happens when ice melts (*it liquefies/turns into water*), when sulphur is heated (*it turns into a gas but does not go through a liquid stage/it sublimes directly to a gas*), when water is used in an electricity generator (*It is heated, it vaporizes, and the steam drives the turbine. It condenses back to water and is re-heated*). Ask for further accounts, such as *What happens when a solid is heated?/when steel is heated?/when a liquid is cooled?* etc. Get students to use sequence markers where there is more than one step.

E The form of the present perfect used with *after* to express a sequential relation is set out here. It is introduced as being similar in meaning to the expressions:
    once+present perfect
    after+gerund
These alternative expressions may be presented on the board before the examples are studied and the exercise is attempted by students. The sentences may be re-written in the three ways as follows:
1   After the steam has left the boiler or reactor, it enters the turbine.
     Once the steam has left the boiler or reactor, it enters the turbine.
     After leaving the boiler or reactor, the steam enters the turbine.
2   After it has condensed, the steam is pumped back to the boiler.
     Once it has condensed, the steam is pumped back to the boiler.
     After condensing, the steam is pumped back to the boiler.

F The expression *depends on* is introduced by means of an example. *The more steam that is used the faster the turbine will rotate* can be re-phrased: *The speed of the turbine depends on the amount of steam used*. All three examples should be completed in the same way. Questions can be asked about the process of electricity generation along the pattern: *What does ... depend on?* Further questions using common examples may be exploited. For example:

    When a wire is stretched, what does the extension depend on?
    The force stretching the wire.

G This part deals with an extended description of the laboratory beam balance, with directions for its use. The passage will need careful study, but students should be able to cope with it as a class exercise, based on language they have met so far. It brings together description, connection of ideas, sequence and instruction.

The first part will need detailed reading in order to decide on which connectives are to be used. The alternatives possible are given in the key below. Words which may be unfamiliar to students, but which could be introduced in context here, are given in brackets. Further practice of *because of/due to* and *as a result of* is given in Unit 8.

The weight of a body is proportional to its mass, and (1) *therefore* (*thus/hence*) the mass of a body can be measured by comparing the earth's pull on it with the pull on a standard mass. This can be done by means of a laboratory beam balance and a set of standard masses (usually called simply 'weights').
(2) *Because/Since* (*Due to the fact that*) laboratory balances are more sensitive than balances used, for instance, in shops, they respond to very small changes in weight. The bearings of the beam and the scale-pan stirrups are made of very hard materials such as agate or synthetic sapphire. (3) *Because of/As a result of* (*Due to*) the design of these bearings and the materials used, they possess very little friction. They also increase the accuracy of the balance, (4) *since/because/as* the sharpness of the knife-edges ensures that the distances between the stirrup bearings and the beam bearing remain constant (5) *as/while* the beam swings. (6) *Since/Because/As* the knife-edges are fragile and easily blunted, they must be protected from damage. (7) *Therefore* (*Thus/Hence*) the beam must be brought to rest before anything is placed on or removed from the pans. This is done by turning the arrestment knob, which lowers the centre bearing and brings the knife-edges out of contact with it and the stirrups.
(8) *Since/Because/As* the scale-pans wear through constant use and cleaning, their mass alters. Balancing screws are (9) *therefore* provided at the ends of the beam. These may be adjusted to compensate for changes in the mass of the pans.

Before students answer the questions, either orally or in writing, the questions themselves may need suitable preparation in class to ensure they are properly understood. They are intended to introduce students to the different forms of questions they can expect to meet, *ie* questions introduced by *in what way, why, how, what*.

Answers will obviously vary, but students should be helped to produce answers which are as clear and straightforward as possible.

As a further exercise, students can be asked to describe the main features of a beam balance in their own words, using the diagram only as a prompt.

exercises

exercise 1

1 Place a record on the turntable.
2 Start the motor.
3 Lift the pick-up head.
4 Move it towards the edge of the record.
5 Position it above the beginning of the record.
6 Lower it carefully onto the record.
7 Lift the head when the pick-up has travelled to the centre of the record.
8 Return it to its original position.
9 Stop the turntable.
10 Remove the record.

exercise 2

1 When current flows in the coil, the core becomes magnetized.
2 Therefore the armature is attracted to the core.
3 Since the hammer is attached to the armature, the bell is struck.
4 When the armature moves towards the core, the contact leaves the adjusting screw.
5 Therefore the circuit is broken.
6 Since there is no current through the coil, there is no magnetic field.
7 Therefore the armature returns to its original position.
8 When the armature touches the screw, the electrical circuit is completed.
9 Thus the sequence is repeated.

(*Thus* may not have been met before, and should be introduced as synonymous with *therefore*.)

exercise 3

1 When measuring temperatures, the type of thermometer used depends on the range of temperatures to be measured.
2 When electricity is generated in a cell, the amount of electricity produced depends on the materials used as electrodes.
3 In an electrical circuit, the deflection of the galvanometer depends on the amount of electricity flowing in the circuit.
4 If a metal bar is heated, the expansion depends on the heat applied.
5 If steam is used to turn a turbine, the speed of rotation of the shaft depends on the amount of steam used.
6 If a turbine is used to drive a generator, the amount of electricity produced depends on the speed of the turbine.
7 If a material is stretched, the extension depends on the force applied.
8 When a material conducts electricity, the quantity of electricity which can pass along it depends on the nature of the material.

drills

drill 1

1 Should I pour some water into the beaker?
   Yes, fill the beaker with water.
2 Should I put the tube into the test-tube?
   Yes, insert the tube into the test-tube.
3 Should I take out the stopper from the container?
   Yes, remove the stopper from the container.
4 Should I see how long the rod is?
   Yes, measure the rod.
5 Should I find out the result of the equation?
   Yes, calculate the result of the equation.
6 Should I join the wire to the terminal?
   Yes, connect the wire to the terminal.
7 Should I look at the reaction?
   Yes, observe the reaction.
8 Should I sketch the apparatus?
   Yes, draw the apparatus.

drill 2

1 What do I do first?
   First you should switch the machine on.
2 Then what do I do?
   Then you should place a full spool of tape on the left-hand spindle.
3 What do I do next?
   Next you should thread the tape through the heads.
4 What do I do after that?
   After that you should join the tape to the take-up spool
5 Then what do I do?
   Then you should press the 'play' button.
6 What do I do after that?
   After that you should adjust the volume control.
7 Then what do I do?
   Then you should listen to the tape.
8 What do I do after that?
   After that you should press the 'stop' button.
9 What do I do next?
   Next you should rewind the tape.
10 And then what do I do?
   Then you should remove the full spool.
11 And after that?
   After that you should switch the machine off.

drill 3

1 A container is first filled with dilute sulphuric acid.
   First fill a container with dilute sulphuric acid.

2 Copper and zinc electrodes are then immersed in the electrolyte.
Then immerse copper and zinc electrodes in the electrolyte.

3 Next, a galvanometer is connected across the electrodes by means of two wires.
Next connect a galvanometer across the electrodes by means of two wires.

4 The reading on the galvanometer scale should then be noted.
Then note the reading on the galvanometer scale.

5 After a time, the action of the acid and the copper should be observed.
After a time, observe the action of the acid and the copper.

6 The electrodes are then removed from the container, and the leads disconnected.
Then remove the electrodes from the container, and disconnect the leads.

7 The copper and zinc electrodes should then be replaced by electrodes of different materials.
Then replace the copper and zinc electrodes by electrodes of different materials.

8 Next, the galvanometer is reconnected.
Next, reconnect the galvanometer.

9 The new value of the galvanometer reading should then be recorded.
Then record the new value of the galvanometer reading.

10 This value should now be compared with the value obtained for copper and zinc electrodes.
Now compare this value with the value obtained for copper and zinc electrodes.

drill **4**

1 What should I do first?
First insert the key into the ignition switch.

2 Yes, I've done that. What should I do next?
Next check the gear and handbrake.

3 Alright, what do I do now?
Now operate the starter.

4 What should I do when the car starts?
When the car starts, engage first gear.

5 What should I do before I drive away?
Before you drive away, check the road.

6 What should I do if the road isn't clear?
If the road isn't clear, wait.

7 What do I do when it's clear?
When it's clear, indicate left or right.

8 Then what do I do?
Then drive away.

drill 5

1   What happens first?
   First, steam is heated in a boiler or reactor.

2   Then what happens?
   Then the steam passes into the turbine.

3   What happens there?
   There the steam drives the turbine shaft.

4   What happens at the same time?
   At the same time, the shaft drives the rotor of the generator.

5   What happens to the steam after passing through the turbine?
   After passing through the turbine, the steam enters the condenser.

6   After it has left the condenser, what happens?
   After it has left the condenser, it is pumped back to the boiler or reactor.

7   What happens when it re-enters the boiler?
   When it re-enters the boiler, it is re-heated.

8   What happens to the electricity once it has been generated?
   Once it has been generated, it is fed into the grid system.

drill 6

1   What does the speed of rotation of the turbine depend on?
   The speed of rotation depends on the amount of steam used.

2   What determines the expansion of a metal when heated?
   The quantity of heat supplied determines the expansion.

3   What does the extension of the wire depend on?
   The extension of the wire depends on the load applied.

4   What determines the voltage produced?
   The electrodes used determine the voltage produced.

5   What does the amount of electricity produced depend on?
   The amount of electricity produced depends on the speed of the turbine.

6   What does the amount of steam produced depend on?
   The amount of steam produced depends on the heat supplied.

7   What does the heat supplied depend on?
   The heat supplied depends on the type of fuel used.

8   What does the rate of cooling depend on?
   The rate of cooling depends on the pressure in the condenser.

activity

The flow chart sets out the sequence of operations involved in making a telephone call from a private telephone. It may be used as the basis of a number of language activities which consolidate the structures covered in this unit. These may include:

Giving simple direct instructions: *Lift the receiver.*
Asking for instruction: *What should I do? What happens if ... ?*
Sequential instruction: *When you've lifted the receiver, you should listen for the dialling tone.*
Indirect instructions in a continuous passage: *The receiver is lifted ...*

The teacher may wish to build up the flow chart together with the students, without the use of the Student's Books. This may be done by preparing a matrix for the flow chart, without any of the lettering, on an overhead projection transparency or the blackboard. The class then discusses together the stages involved in making a telephone call, and the stages are entered onto the chart.

unit 7

classwork

SECTION 1 **cause and reason**

A The teacher may wish to present and practise the use of *why* and *because* in a general context before beginning this section.

Students use the two tables to ask and answer questions about **reason**. The tables can then be used to make statements of **cause,** as in the example. The first part of each statement is given.

1   Like magnetic poles repel each other because there is a magnetic force between them.
2   Gases expand when they are heated because they absorb heat energy.
3   Glass breaks when it is hit because it is extremely brittle.
4   A balloon filled with helium floats because helium is lighter than air.
5   Copper can be stretched easily because it is very ductile.
6   When a copper wire is connected to a cell, it conducts electricity because there is a movement of electrons through it.

B This is a class exercise on the formation of questions and answers using *why* and *because*. The complete questions and answers may be written up, if desired.

1   Why is copper used in electrical connections?
    Because it is an extremely good conductor.
2   Why does a suction pad stick to a flat surface?
    Because there is no air between the pad and the surface.
3   Why is steel tempered?
    Because it is brittle when hardened.
4   Why does heat pass along a conductor?
    Because the molecules of the conductor vibrate.
5   Why doesn't rubber break when it is hit?
    Because it is extremely resilient.
6   Why does the earth have day and night?
    Because it revolves about its own axis.
7   Why is mercury used in laboratory thermometers?
    Because it has a high boiling point.
8   Why is hydrogen dangerous?
    Because it is highly inflammable.

The exercise should be repeated, making single statements of reason, as shown in the example.

C The expression of cause is introduced. This is done by including the verb *cause* in statements. The examples should be completed.

Hitting a piece of glass *will cause it to* break.
Applying a tensile force to a wire *will cause it to* extend.
Cooling a metal bar *will cause it to* contract.

The statements of cause may be completed in the following way, the class discussing, if necessary, what the actions will cause.

1   Heating water to 100°C will cause it to boil.
2   Cooling water to 0°C will cause it to freeze.
3   Filling a balloon with air will cause it to expand.
4   Holding a piece of wood in a flame will cause it to burn.
5   Placing sugar in hot coffee will cause it to dissolve.
6   Puncturing a balloon will cause it to burst.

When a pronoun is used in a sentence, there is sometimes more than one noun the pronoun could be replacing. A simple example demonstrates this problem. Students should be aware of this problem, so that they can avoid confusion wherever possible.

The statements of cause are completed, care being taken to avoid ambiguity. The class should discuss which sentences are likely to be ambiguous if the pronoun is used, and the sentences worded so as to avoid this. Clearly, confusion is less likely to occur in sentences such as No 1, where *it* is unlikely to refer to the hammer.

Suitable ways of completing the sentences are:

1   Hitting a piece of glass with a hammer will cause it to break/shatter, etc.
2   Dropping an egg on the floor will cause it to break.
3   Placing blue litmus paper in an acid will cause the litmus paper to turn red.
4   Striking a match on a matchbox will cause the match to light.
5   Bringing the north pole of a magnet near the north pole of a suspended magnet will cause the suspended magnet to turn.
6   Passing a current through a coil around a soft iron core will cause the core to become magnetized.
7   Lighting a cigarette with a match will cause the cigarette to burn.
8   Sucking liquid through a straw will cause the liquid to rise up the straw.

D The expressions *cause, bring about, result in* followed by a noun group are introduced. The table should be used for practice in forming this structure. Suitable sentences would be:

Heating hydrogen will cause/bring about/result in an explosion.
Cooling a gas will cause/bring about/result in a change in pressure.
Splitting an atom will cause/bring about/result in a release of energy.
Heating a copper bar will cause/bring about/result in an increase in volume.
Completing an electric circuit will cause/bring about/result in a flow of current.

The patterns shown should be used to ask and answer questions about cause and result, using the phrases on the left-hand side of the table.

E The passage and diagram should be studied, new words and expressions being explained. Students should then practise asking and answering questions about the principle of a safety match, using the question and answer patterns given.

The process of striking a safety match is summarized and students should describe the principle, making statements of cause and result.

SECTION 2 comparison and contrast

A The teacher may wish to introduce the idea of **comparison**, using suitable objects and examples and stating their differences and similarities, before the examples in the book are studied. The words *whereas, while* and *whilst* can be introduced in this way in a general context before the exercise is attempted. The statements of comparison should be completed by the class, using these words.

1   Copper is a conductor, whereas/while/whilst glass is an insulator.
2   Iron is a solid, whereas/while/whilst mercury is a liquid.
3   Carbon is an element, whereas/while/whilst carbon dioxide is a compound.
4   Iron is cheap, whereas/while/whilst gold is expensive.
5   Water is colourless, whereas/while/whilst sulphur is yellow.
6   Zinc is a solid, whereas/while/whilst hydrogen is a gas.
7   Aluminium is light, whereas/while/whilst lead is heavy.
8   Paper is weak, whereas/while/whilst steel is strong.
9   Wool is soft, whereas/while/whilst wood is hard.
10   Protons are positively charged, whereas/while/whilst electrons are negatively charged.

The note at the end of this exercise introduces the idea of contrast, which is developed further in **B**.

B Question patterns asking about **difference** are introduced. The patterns given in these examples may first be presented and practised in a general context before studying the notes and examples. The example statements of difference should be studied, and the notes used as the basis for similar statements. The class should try to think of as many differences as possible between the things named.

C The idea of **exception** is introduced, leading to the use of *although* in statements of exception. This construction may be presented in a general context, before the statements are studied in a scientific context.

The expressions *though* and *even though* are introduced as being similar in meaning to *although*.

D The table should be used to make statements with *although, even though* and *though*. The statements should be correct in meaning.

Although/Even though/Though carbon dioxide is a colourless and odourless gas, it can be detected with lime water.

Although/Even though/Though steel is brittle when hardened, it can be toughened by tempering.

Although/Even though/Though glass is brittle, it can be made more resilient by toughening.

Although/Even though/Though copper is expensive, it is widely used as a conductor.

Although/Even though/Though alcohol thermometers are inexpensive, they are not widely used for laboratory work.

Although/Even though/Though energy can be converted into other forms, it cannot be created or destroyed.

E The alternative order of words in statements with *although*, *though* and *even though* is introduced. The table should again be used to make statements, using the alternative word order.

F The expression *however* is introduced, and should be inserted into the example sentences. The notes can then be used to make pairs of sentences.

1   Mercury is a metal. However, it is liquid at room temperature.
2   Copper is ductile. However, it will break if subjected to a high tensile force.
3   Glass is extremely brittle. However, it can be toughened by using a special process.
4   The particles of an atom are charged. However, the complete atom does not have a charge.
5   In a simple cell, sulphate ions and copper ions are discharged. However, copper ions are discharged more easily than sulphate ions.
6   Metals contract when cooled to 0°C. However, water expands when cooled from 4°C to 0°C.
7   Air does not conduct heat very well. However, air can be heated by convection.
8   An atom is extremely small. However, it consists of much smaller particles.

The alternative word order of statements with *however* is introduced, and the above exercise may be repeated, re-ordering the words as in the example.

G The examples summarize the connectors and statements of comparison, contrast and exception presented in this section.

The statements may be completed as follows. (Nb *while* may sometimes be used with a similar function to *although*. This use is not given in the key, as it is left to the teacher to decide whether to introduce this use here.)

1   *Although/Even though/Though* the quantity of carbon dioxide in the earth's atmosphere is relatively small, the gas is essential for supporting life. Plants require carbon dioxide, and they remove it from the air in a

process known as photosynthesis. *Although/Even though/Though* carbon dioxide is therefore being removed from the atmosphere continuously, it is *however* continuously replaced by animal and plant respiration and decay.

2   Nitrogen is essential for life, since it is needed in the formation of proteins, which are vital constituents of animal and plant cells. *However*, atmospheric nitrogen cannot be used directly by plants and animals, *although/even though/though* it is an essential element. Men and animals obtain their nitrogen by eating plants and other animals, *but/while/whilst/whereas* plants absorb soluble nitrogen compounds from the soil, through their roots.

SECTION 3   **similarity**

A The teacher may wish to present or elicit simple statements of **similarity**, using suitable examples, before proceeding to a study of this section.

The words *similar* and *similarity* are introduced. The table can be used to elicit the similarities between the substances mentioned. As many similarities as possible should be elicited from the class.

B The construction *both ... and ...* is introduced. The notes should be used as the basis for statements of similarity:

1   Aluminium is both strong and light.
2   Copper is both a good conductor of heat and a good conductor of electricity.
3   Solids have both definite shape and definite volume.
4   Nylon is both tough and inexpensive.
5   An electric current in a wire has both a heating effect and a magnetic effect.
6   The nucleus of an atom has both protons and neutrons.
7   A vector quantity has both direction and magnitude.

The constructions *not only ... but ... as well* and *not only ... but also ...* are introduced. They can then be used to produce statements using the same sets of notes as above.

C The constructions *either ... or ...* and *neither ... nor ...* are introduced, together with the concept of **alternatives**. The notes should be used as the basis for statements with *either ... or ...* and *neither ... nor*.

D The passage contains the various expressions of contrast and comparison which have been introduced so far. It should be studied in detail, and may be used as the basis for asking and answering questions comparing and contrasting states of matter. Questions may be written on the board if students have difficulty with them orally. In addition to asking questions which the students answer, the teacher may prompt students into asking each other questions on the passage. Suggested questions might include:

What are the characteristics of a material in a solid state/a liquid state/a gaseous state?
How is it possible to change the state of materials?
What happens when water is cooled/heated?
How do different materials differ in their changes of state?

Students may then be asked to reconstruct the statements without using their books, given prompts such as:

Outline the properties of a material in a solid state/in a liquid state/in a gaseous state.

exercises

exercise 1 Some differences in wording are possible.
1 Atmospheric pressure.
2 A tube.
3 Air is removed from the tube.
4 Because the atmospheric pressure acting down on the liquid is greater than the pressure inside the tube.
5 Because the end of the tube outside the container is below the level of the liquid inside it.
6 It causes the liquid to flow out of the tube.
7 The liquid will cease to flow along the tube.

exercise 2 Some differences in wording and word order are possible.
1 Aluminium is fairly strong, whilst copper is very strong.
2 Aluminium is fairly cheap, whereas copper is not very cheap.
3 Aluminium is not very easy to solder. Copper, however, is easy to solder.
4 Although copper is very strong, it is not very light.
5 Though aluminium is fairly cheap, it is not very easy to solder.
6 Although copper is a very good conductor, it is not very cheap.
7 Copper has a very low resistance. However, it is not very light.
8 Aluminium is a good conductor, while copper is a very good conductor.
9 Aluminium has a fairly low resistance, but copper has a very low resistance.
10 Aluminium has a very high corrosion resistance, whereas copper has a fairly high corrosion resistance.

exercise 3 Some differences in word order are possible.
1 Ions can be either negatively-charged or positively-charged.
2 Steel can be not only hardened but also tempered.
3 Hydrogen can be produced both by iron and hydrochloric acid and by zinc and hydrochloric acid.
4 Metals can be either ferrous or non-ferrous.
5 Electric current can be either alternating current or direct current.
6 Electricity can both heat a wire and have a magnetic effect.
7 Energy can be neither created nor destroyed.
8 Vector quantities have not only magnitude but also direction.
9 Gold is neither cheap nor common.
10 Paper is neither strong nor rigid.

drills

drill 1

1 Why is alcohol often used in thermometers?
  Because it is less expensive than mercury.

2 Why are copper and aluminium used for electrical connections?
  Because they are good conductors.

3 Why does glass shatter when it is hit?
  Because it is extremely brittle.

4 Why is mercury used in laboratory thermometers?
  Because it has a high boiling point.

5 Why doesn't rubber break when it is dropped?
  Because it is very resilient.

6 Why do gases expand when heated?
  Because they absorb heat energy.

7 Why are some matches called 'safety matches'?
  Because they only strike against special surfaces.

8 Why do oxygen and sulphur generate heat in a match?
  Because they react chemically.

9 Why does copper bend very easily?
  Because it is very ductile.

10 Why are porcelain and glass often used in electrical work?
  Because they are good insulators.

drill 2

1 What will dropping a piece of glass do?
  It will cause it to break.

2 What will stretching a length of wire do?
  It will cause it to extend.

3 What will cooling water to 0°C do?
  It will cause it to freeze.

4 What will heating a block of metal do?
  It will cause it to expand.

5 What will striking a match do?
  It will cause it to light.

6 What will filling a balloon with air do?
  It will cause it to expand.

7 What will puncturing a balloon do?
  It will cause it to explode.

8 What will placing sugar in hot coffee do?
  It will cause it to dissolve.

9 What will heating water to 100°C do?
  It will cause it to boil.

10 What will putting acid on blue litmus paper do?
  It will cause it to turn red.

drill 3

1   Are both rubber and glass resilient?
    No, rubber is resilient, whereas glass is brittle.

2   Are air and oxygen both mixtures?
    No, air is a mixture, but oxygen is an element.

3   Are both copper and glass conductors?
    No, copper is a conductor, while glass is an insulator.

4   Are iron and water both elements?
    No, iron is an element, whilst water is a compound.

5   Are copper and mercury both solids?
    No, copper is a solid, but mercury is a liquid.

6   Are aluminium and porcelain both insulators?
    No, porcelain is an insulator, whereas aluminium is a conductor.

7   Are steel and iron both elements?
    No, iron is an element, but steel is a compound.

8   Are both glass and rubber brittle?
    No, glass is brittle, while rubber is resilient.

9   Are glass and wood both transparent?
    No, glass is transparent, whereas wood is opaque.

10 Are water and milk both colourless?
    No, water is colourless, but milk is white.

drill 4

1   Mercury is a metal. Is it normally a solid?
    No, although mercury is a metal, it isn't normally a solid.

2   The particles of an atom have charges. Is the atom itself charged?
    No, although the particles of an atom have charges, the atom itself isn't charged.

3   Aluminium is a good conductor. Is it very easy to solder?
    No, although aluminium is a good conductor, it isn't very easy to solder.

4   Energy can be converted. Can it be destroyed?
    No, although energy can be converted, it can't be destroyed.

5   Alcohol thermometers are cheap. Are they normally used in laboratories?
    No, although alcohol thermometers are cheap, they aren't normally used in laboratories.

6   Aluminium exists as an ore. Is it easy to extract pure aluminium?
    No, although aluminium exists as an ore, it isn't easy to extract pure aluminium.

7   Aluminium is quite strong. Is it very heavy?
    No, although aluminium is quite strong, it isn't very heavy.

8   Diamonds are a form of carbon. Are they cheap?
    No, although diamonds are a form of carbon, they aren't cheap.

drill 5

1 Aluminium is strong, isn't it?
Yes, it's not only strong but light as well.

2 Copper's very malleable.
Yes, it's not only very malleable but also very ductile.

3 Water's colourless, isn't it?
Yes, it's not only colourless but also odourless.

4 Solids have definite shape.
Yes, they not only have definite shape but definite volume as well.

5 Nylon's extremely tough, isn't it?
Yes, it's not only extremely tough but relatively inexpensive as well.

6 Copper's a good conductor of heat.
Yes, it's not only a good conductor of heat but also of electricity.

7 Vector quantities have magnitude.
Yes, they have not only magnitude but also direction.

8 An atom consists of electrons.
Yes, it consists of not only electrons but a nucleus as well.

drill 6

1 Gases have both definite volume and definite shape, don't they?
No, gases have neither definite volume nor definite shape.

2 Air and oxygen are both compounds, aren't they?
No, neither air nor oxygen are compounds.

3 Rubber and polythene are both brittle, aren't they?
No, neither rubber nor polythene are brittle.

4 Both protons and neutrons are negatively charged, aren't they?
No, neither protons nor neutrons are negatively charged.

5 Gold and copper both have high melting-points, don't they?
No, neither gold nor copper have high-melting points.

6 Aluminium and steel are magnetic, aren't they?
No, neither aluminium nor steel are magnetic.

7 Carbon dioxide and nitrogen both have a strong smell, don't they?
No, neither carbon dioxide nor nitrogen have a strong smell.

8 Glass is both pliable and resilient, isn't it?
No, glass is neither pliable nor resilient.

9 Wood and paper are both conductors, aren't they?
No, neither wood nor paper are conductors.

10 Glass has both high tensile strength and a high melting-point, doesn't it?
No, glass has neither high tensile strength nor a high melting-point.

activity

The class should study the diagram and the sequence in block diagram form in the Student's Book. These illustrate the sequence of events in the setting-up of a convection current in a room. The class should be able to draw up a complete description of the sequence simply from a discussion of the diagrams. The description should include expressions of cause and result.

The teacher may wish to write up the description with the students, have students write this individually, or have individual students describe the whole sequence of cause orally, using the notes and diagram.

A suitable account of the process of convection might be as follows:

Air near the source of heat becomes warm through conduction. This causes it to become less dense, and it therefore rises. As it rises, it gets further away from the source of heat, and this results in it cooling. When the air cools, it becomes more dense, and this causes it to fall. Since air near the heat source is rising, the cool air is then able to replace the air near the heat source, where it is warmed. A complete repetition of the convection cycle is therefore brought about.

unit 8

classwork

SECTION 1 **likely or probable result**

A The teacher may begin the presentation of the expression of **probable result**, using suitable examples, before proceeding to a study of this section.

Examples of statements of definite result are given in the Student's Book. The students will by now be familiar with such statements. An example of a situation is then given in which the definite result cannot be stated.

Ask what will happen if certain actions are performed. For example:

What will happen if I bend this ruler?
                              stand on this piece of chalk?
                              drop this pencil?
                              drop this lighted match?
                              pour acid over the table?
                              put my hand on an electric wire?

Students should reply to these questions with statements using *is likely to* and *will probably*.

B The diagram and the passage should be studied carefully. The passage states the likely or probable result of an action. Words such as *fracture*, *dangerous* and *immediately* should be introduced if they are not already known. Using the situation illustrated in the passage, the structure of a sentence with *unless* can be introduced:

The cylinder is likely to fracture *unless* the pressure is reduced.

Students' attention should be focussed onto this word and to the way in which it is used to express condition. Similar statements with *is likely to* and *unless* may be made to describe the situations listed:

1   The wire is likely to melt unless the current is reduced.
2   The cylinder is likely to explode unless the pressure is reduced.
3   The liquid is likely to boil unless the heat is reduced.
4   The wire is likely to undergo permanent deformation unless the tensile force is reduced.
5   The plastic is likely to melt unless the temperature is reduced.
6   The wood is likely to catch light unless the strength of the flame is reduced.
7   The cylinder is likely to fracture unless the pressure is reduced.
8   The bar is likely to bend unless the downward force is reduced.

C The structure: adjective+*enough* is introduced with the examples *low enough* and *high enough*. Statements containing a condition are introduced, using the construction with *provided*.

The notes should be used to form similar statements of condition, on the same pattern as the examples.

1   Steel will stretch provided it is subjected to a high enough tensile force.

2 Oxygen will freeze provided it is cooled to a low enough temperature.
3 Helium will liquefy provided it is subjected to a high enough pressure.
4 Rubber will melt provided it is heated to a high enough temperature.
5 Sulphur will vaporize provided it is heated to a high enough temperature.

D The statement of condition is extended to general statements of result. The statements 1–5 should be re-phrased, using *provided* and *enough*.

1 When a metal bar is stretched, it will extend provided the force is large enough.
2 When carbon dioxide is cooled, it will solidify provided the temperature is low enough.
3 When copper is heated, it will melt provided the temperature is high enough.
4 When salt is placed in water, it will dissolve provided the water is warm enough.
5 When helium is compressed, it will become liquid provided the pressure is high enough.

E The statement of likely or probable outcome is extended to the use of *should* and *ought to*. The expressions *it should do* and *it ought to* are introduced as indicating that a given result is considered likely to occur. The example of the battery and bulb is given. Three further examples are given, together with the conditions under which something is thought likely to happen. Taking suitable objects, the teacher should ask the class if certain actions will have the results suggested. For example:

Will this radio come on if I press this button?
Yes, it ought to/should do, provided there's a battery in it/it's plugged in/it's not broken.

Other questions which might be used are:

Will this liquid boil if I heat it?
Will this match light if I strike it?
Will this door open if I push/pull it?

The teacher should supply further questions in a similar form, with objects in the room. If desired, the negative forms *No, it ought not to/No, it shouldn't do* may be introduced, drawing attention to the appropriate intonation pattern. Questions may be asked in a similar way, this time eliciting the negative forms. For example,

Will this chair break if I stand on it?
No, it ought not to/shouldn't do, provided it's strong enough/you're careful/you're not too heavy.

SECTION 2 **hypothetical result**

A Hypothetical conditional statements may be presented in a general context before this section is studied, if desired.

A summary is given in the Student's Book of statements of firm prediction (conditional type 1). Conditional type 2 is introduced with an explanation to the effect that this form is used if the action is not definitely going to be performed. It is used to state the result of a **hypothetical** action. Explain that you are not really going to throw a stone at the window, take hold of an electric wire, pour concentrated acid on the table, etc, but say what *would* happen if these things *were done*.

Examples of hypothetical condition are given in this part, together with the question form *What would happen if I ... ?* The notes should be used to make questions and statements of hypothetical condition, referring to the situations in the illustrations.

1   Q. What would happen if I heated this piece of aluminium to 1,800°C?
    A. It would melt.
2   Q. What would happen if I placed zinc in dilute hydrochloric acid?
    A. The zinc would react with the acid.
3   Q. What would happen if I stretched this copper wire beyond its elastic limit?
    A. It would undergo permanent deformation.
4   Q. What would happen if I held some glass and some wood together in a flame?
    A. The glass would melt and the wood would burn.

B The objects in the table—a stone, a ruler, chalk, paper, elastic—should be supplied by the teacher so that they can be handed to the students. Students can then ask *What would happen if I ... ?* This relates the hypothetical situation directly to the object concerned (*this stone, this piece of paper* etc). The answers to these questions should take the form *The ... would ...* or *It would ...*

C Passive statements of hypothetical condition are introduced by illustrating the transition from statements containing 'I' to statements with the construction *If ... were ...* Several examples of statements with this construction are given, and these should be studied by the class. The questions from the table in **B** can also be turned into the passive.

Statements of hypothetical condition with *probably* are introduced, indicating the likely result of a hypothetical action. The sentence form *What do you think would happen if ... ?* is introduced, and the notes can be used to ask questions in this form. The questions are answered using the word *probably*. Model answers are given below, but other versions are possible.

1   What do you think would happen if a cylinder of hydrogen were heated?
    It would probably explode.
2   What do you think would happen if salt were added to water?
    The salt would probably dissolve.
3   What do you think would happen if a thin copper wire were subjected to a high tensile force?
    It would probably undergo permanent deformation.

4   What do you think would happen if a piece of glass were heated and then cooled quickly?
    It would probably shatter.
5   What would happen if carbon dioxide were 'poured' over a fire?
    The fire would probably go out.
6   What do you think would happen if a bar of steel were bent by an extremely large force?
    It would probably fracture.
7   What do you think would happen if too high a current were passed through a coil?
    The coil would probably overheat.
8   What do you think would happen if a piece of wood were heated to too high a temperature?
    It would probably burn.

Note   The passive in these sentences is formed with *were* only in order to simplify the structure as much as possible for the student. But obviously *was* may be used in the 3rd person singular. For instance, the following sentence may be written in either of the two ways: *If a piece of glass was/were heated and then cooled quickly, it would probably shatter.*

D   Further connectors used to indicate the reason for a given result are introduced. These include *because* and *since*, which have been met before. The connectors are

owing to	because
due to	since
as a result of	as
because of	

    The teacher may choose to give other examples of these expressions, or elicit answers from the class to questions about various causes. This may be done with reference to everyday as well as scientific examples. The two groups of connectors introduced here have their use restricted in different ways. *Due to, as a result of, because of* are used before a noun group; *because, since, as* are used before a clause. In their books, students are asked if they can identify the difference in usage. The exercise in **C** can then be repeated, students extending their answers to include a statement of cause or reason introduced by one of the connectors above.

E   The passage gives an account of the action of a simple barometer. It may be treated as follows. Teacher and students read the passage together, new words and expressions are explained, and the teacher asks intensive comprehension questions. Students may be asked to read sections of the passage aloud. A further exploitation would be for students to close their books, the class then building up the diagram and the description together from memory.

Note   In the expression *the pressure due to the column of liquid, due to* is used in its prepositional sense, relating to pressure, and is not a connector as taught in **D**.

F The way in which the gerund can be used to replace the *if* form in statements of hypothetical condition is introduced: *Using water in a barometer would result in too long a column of liquid.* (*nb* the contracted form *too long a* = a column which is too long) *Setting up a barometer on top of a mountain would result in a shorter column of mercury than at ground level.*

The following statements may be made:

Adding zinc to hydrochloric acid would cause/result in/bring about a chemical reaction.
Igniting a cylinder of hydrogen would cause/result in/bring about an explosion.
Immersing iron in water would cause/result in/bring about corrosion.
Stretching copper wire would cause/result in/bring about an extension.

The actions would have the following results (these examples will need to be completed as a class exercise, with the differences in structure being pointed out):

1   Plunging a glowing splint into a gas-jar of oxygen would cause the splint to catch fire/result in the splint catching fire.
2   Blowing too much air into a balloon would cause the balloon to burst/result in the balloon bursting.
3   Passing carbon dioxide through lime water would cause the lime water to turn cloudy/result in the lime water turning cloudy.
4   Splitting an atom would cause energy to be released/result in energy being released.
5   Dropping a test-tube onto a hard surface would cause the test-tube to shatter/result in the test-tube shattering.

SECTION 3   **suggesting possible cause and result**

A The teacher may wish to begin the presentation from the starting-point of statement of probable result, and then introduce results which cannot be predicted with any certainty. It will then be necessary to introduce the word *perhaps* to indicate a possible result.

In the example given in the Student's Book, a definite or probable result cannot be stated. It is therefore necessary to indicate a possible result, introducing this with *perhaps*. Students should ask questions from the table and supply suitable possible results, using the pattern: *I don't know. Perhaps it would* ... Suitable answers would be:

I don't know. Perhaps it would react.
dissolve.
explode.
liquefy.
snap.
melt.

The teacher may supply further questions and ask the students to think of more. These could be from everyday as well as scientific situations.

B *Might* is introduced in statements of possible result: *It might burn, or it might melt*. The exercise in **A** should be repeated, using *might*.

C *May* is introduced as being synonymous with *might* in this sense. Examples are given of statements using *may* and *might*. These should be studied by the class. Students should then ask and answer similar questions about things in the room. For example:

Will this chair break if I stand on it?
It may do.
Will this bottle break if it's dropped?
It might do.

D *Could* is introduced as being synonymous with *may* and *might* when used in this sense. An example of a situation and a statement with *may*, *might* or *could* is given. Similar statements can be made from the situations listed:

1   If the substance is not removed, it may/might/could react with the acid.
2   If the connections aren't altered, the transistor may/might/could be ruined.
3   If the temperature is raised any more, the material may/might/could burn.
4   If the force is not removed soon, the metal may/might/could undergo permanent deformation.
5   If the plastic container isn't moved away from the source of heat, it may/might/could melt.
6   If the crack isn't sealed, the gas may/might/could escape.
7   If the glass bottle isn't moved away from the edge of the shelf, it may/might/could fall.
8   If the liquid isn't removed from the container, it may/might/could solidify.

The exercise may be repeated using *unless* to replace *if ... not*.

E Statements with *otherwise* are introduced. The statements in **D** are rephrased so as to include *otherwise*.

1   The substance must be removed, otherwise it may/might/could react with the acid.
2   The connections must be altered, otherwise the transistor may/might/could be ruined.
3   The temperature mustn't be raised any more, otherwise the material may/might/could burn.
4   The force must be removed soon, otherwise the metal may/might/could undergo permanent deformation.
5   The plastic container must be moved away from the source of heat, otherwise it may/might/could melt.
6   The crack must be sealed, otherwise the gas may/might/could escape.

7   The glass bottle must be moved away from the edge of the shelf, otherwise it may/might/could fall.

8   The liquid must be removed from the container, otherwise it may/might/could solidify.

F The use of *may*, *might* and *could* to suggest possible reason is introduced.

The combination of *may*, *might* or *could be* with the connectors *due to*, *because of* and *because* is introduced. The table should be used to make statements expressing possible cause, relating to the situation described.

In these tables, words such as *flat* (meaning weak or 'dead' when applied to batteries), *faulty*, *damaged* will have to be explained. They are very frequently used when discussing possible faults.

G A situation is outlined in which suggestions have to be made as to the cause of a break-down in a car. This exercise takes the form of a dialogue (between A and B). Various utterances are possible for each line of the dialogue, and so the following method is suggested for conducting the exercise. An example of one of the possibilities of the dialogue is given (read by the teacher or played on tape):

A: There's something wrong with my car.
B: Oh, what's the trouble?
A: Well, it won't start.
B: I see. It could be because there's no petrol in the tank.
A: No, it can't be the petrol because I've checked it.

Pairs of students then practise the dialogue, suggesting various reasons why the car won't start. After this has been practised sufficiently, students should close their books and try conducting the dialogue without the notes. The teacher may wish to suggest a similar situation in which something doesn't work (a telephone, radio, television, tape recorder, etc). The students then build up a similar dialogue together, the whole class suggesting possible reasons for the fault. The list of possible causes is then written up, and pairs of students conduct the dialogue as with the printed exercise.

exercises

exercise 1

1 It will probably break, provided the tensile force is large/great/high enough.
2 It will probably solidify, provided the temperature is low enough.
3 It will probably become very hot, provided the current is large/high/great enough.
4 It will probably catch fire, provided the flame is hot enough.
5 It will probably withstand the shock, provided it is resilient enough.
6 It will probably become a liquid, provided the pressure is great/high enough.
7 It will probably light, provided the battery is powerful enough.
8 It will probably reflect the heat, provided it is clean and shiny enough.

exercise 2

1 If carbon dioxide were poured over a fire, the fire would probably go out because carbon dioxide cannot support combustion.
2 If a high current were passed through a wire, the wire would probably melt because of the heating effect of the current.
3 If salt were added to water, it would probably dissolve since salt is soluble in water.
4 If iron were left in contact with water, it would probably corrode as a result of oxidation.
5 If a copper wire were subjected to a tensile force, it would probably extend as copper is fairly elastic.
6 If a test tube of hydrogen were ignited, it would probably explode because hydrogen is extremely inflammable.
7 If a polythene container were placed near a source of heat, it would probably melt because of the low melting point of polythene.
8 If a glass bottle were dropped onto the floor, it would probably shatter since glass is extremely brittle.

exercise 3

1 The material must not be exposed to water, otherwise it may/might/could corrode.
2 The transistor must not be wrongly connected, otherwise it may/might/could be damaged.
3 A high current must not be passed through the wire, otherwise it may/might/could overheat.
4 The liquid must not be cooled too quickly, otherwise it may/might/could solidify.
5 The plastic must not be too near a source of heat, otherwise it may/might/could melt.
6 The gas must not be exposed to a naked flame, otherwise it may/might/could burn.

7 The container must not be damaged, otherwise gas may/might/could escape.

8 The material must not be stretched, otherwise it may/might/could undergo permanent deformation.

drills

drill 1

1   Gas is being pumped into a cylinder to a very high pressure. What is likely to happen?
It's likely to explode.

2   Water is being cooled to a low temperature. What will probably happen?
It will probably freeze (or solidify).

3   A wire is stretched by a high tensile force. What is likely to happen?
It's likely to snap.

4   Salt is stirred into some water. What will probably happen?
It will probably dissolve.

5   A high current is being passed through a very thin wire. What is likely to happen?
It's likely to overheat (or melt).

6   Some plastic is standing near a very strong source of heat. What is likely to happen?
It's likely to melt.

7   A piece of wood is being held in a flame. What will probably happen?
It will probably catch light.

8   Oxygen is being cooled to an extremely low temperature. What is likely to happen?
It's likely to liquefy.

drill 2

1   Will this lamp light up if I connect the battery?
Yes, it should do, provided the battery is powerful enough.

2   Will this gas explode?
No, not unless it's heated strongly.

3   Will this metal wire extend if a tensile force is applied to it?
Yes, it should do, provided the force is strong enough.

4   Will this container break very easily?
No, not unless it's subjected to a violent shock.

5   Will these chemicals react together?
No, not unless they are heated strongly.

6   Will this metal melt if the temperature is raised?
Yes, it should do, provided the temperature is high enough.

7   Will this helium balloon burst?
No, not unless it's punctured.

8   Will this solid dissolve if it's placed in water?
Yes, it should do, provided the water's warm enough.

drill 3

1   What would happen if zinc and dilute hydrochloric acid were placed together in a container?
They would react.

2   What would happen if a piece of glass were dropped onto the floor?
It would probably shatter.

3   What would happen if a material were stretched beyond its elastic limit?
     It would undergo permanent deformation.

4   What would happen if a piece of copper were heated?
     It would expand.

5   What would happen if a high current were passed through a thin wire?
     It would probably melt.

6   What would happen if a cylinder of hydrogen were heated?
     It would probably explode.

7   What would happen if two magnetic north poles were brought near to each other?
     They would repel each other.

8   What would happen if pieces of glass and copper were heated to a very high temperature?
     They would melt.

drill 4

1   Copper isn't light enough to be used in overhead power cables.
     No, if it were lighter it would probably be used more in overhead power cables.

2   Gold is too expensive to be used as a conductor.
     Yes, if it were less expensive it would probably be used more as a conductor.

3   At the moment, batteries aren't powerful enough to be used in electric cars.
     No, if they were more powerful they would probably be used more in electric cars.

4   Ordinary glass isn't tough enough to be used in laboratory work.
     No, if it were tougher it would probably be used more in laboratory work.

5   Hydrogen is too inflammable to be used in many experiments.
     Yes, if it were less inflammable it would probably be used more in experiments.

6   Hardened steel is too brittle to be used before being tempered.
     Yes, if it were less brittle it would probably be used more before being tempered.

7   Porcelain isn't resilient enough to be used as an insulator in some applications.
     No, if it were more resilient it would probably be used more as an insulator in some applications.

8   Ordinary batteries are too heavy to be used in electric vehicles.
     Yes, if they were less heavy they would probably be used more in electric vehicles.

drill 5

A: Will the bell ring if I press the switch?
B: Well, it ought to, but it won't.

A: Oh—what do you think is wrong with it?
B: I don't know. Have you got any ideas?
A: Well, there might be something wrong with the bell.
B: No, it couldn't be the bell—it's a new one.
A: Oh, well, perhaps the wiring's not correct or the connections are broken.
B: No, the wiring is alright, I've checked it with the diagram. And if the connections were broken we'd be able to see them.
A: Do you think the switch could be faulty?
B: It might be—but it worked alright before.
A: Well, in that case, it can only be one thing.
B: The battery?
A: Yes. If you change the battery the circuit ought to work.
B: Yes, that should do it. I've got a new battery here. Let's try it. I'll just disconnect the old one. Right, there we are. Now let's see ...
(*ring*)

drill 6   Dialogue—Part II   The complete dialogue in Drill 5 is repeated. Students speak with the second speaker. The dialogue is then repeated with only the first speaker's utterances. Students speak in the pauses, taking the part of the second speaker.

activity

This activity is outlined in the Student's Book. Students are asked to discuss what they could do and what they ought to do or should do in the various situations outlined. This will involve students in making statements of possibility, for example *You could ...*, *You might be able to ...*, and suggestions: *Perhaps you could ...* as well as advising: *You ought to ...*, *You should ...* The activity may be handled in a number of ways. It could be started by the class discussing one particular situation together, trying to work out a solution. Here the teacher and some of the students may like to make the situation more complicated by putting forward objections as to why a particular suggestion cannot be used. For example, in No 1 the suggestion *You could call the fire brigade to help you* may be made. The objection *But I live in the country and there's no telephone for five miles* could be put forward. Individual students may then be asked to try to solve individual problems, the rest of the class again putting forward objections.

The problem-solving situations may be turned into short dialogues (as in Drills 5 and 6). For example,

A: What's the matter?
B: I must be up early tomorrow, but I haven't got an alarm clock.
A: What are you going to do?
B: I don't know. What do you suggest?

The teacher supplies new words and phrases as these are required by the students. These may be written on the board so that they can be incorporated into dialogues by the other students. The teacher may wish to supplement the list of situations given with further examples, either of a technical or everyday nature. If desired, the class could then be presented with a piece of apparatus or machinery or a device which is not working properly (for instance, a transistor radio). The class must then discuss what could be wrong with it, and how it could be put right.

unit 9

classwork

SECTION 1 **reporting actions**

This section deals with description of experimental procedure and observed results and involves the past simple passive.

A A series of instructions for carrying out an experiment is given. The diagram shows the apparatus used. Students should be able to read and understand most of this text without too much help from the teacher, since it contains direct instructions, which have been studied before. Some of the vocabulary and expressions may need introducing, for example *regular intervals, approach, plot a graph, attempt to deduce*, and so on. The teacher may wish the students to read these instructions alone and then study them together, or to begin by reading them to the class, followed by students reading them aloud with the teacher asking questions after each instruction.

When the text has been studied, students may be asked to outline the series of instructions for carrying out the experiment, without looking at their books.

Students' attention is drawn to the presence of words of instruction (the term *imperative* may be introduced if desired) in the passage. They are then asked to go back over the passage, underlining all the words of instruction they can identify.

B Examples are given in the Student's Book (which the teacher may wish to supplement) outlining how the transition may be made from statements of direct instruction (telling the reader what to do) to statements reporting completed actions (telling the reader what was done). In this way, the past simple passive is introduced.

The instructions in **A** may be converted into a report of an experiment by placing the words of instruction (underlined by the students) in the past simple passive. The series of statements should then appear in the following form:

1   Some ice *was crushed* and *mixed* with salt to form a freezing mixture.
2   This mixture *was placed* in a large container.
3   A small amount of hot water *was poured* into a calorimeter.
4   The calorimeter *was* then *inserted* into the freezing mixture.
5   The water *was allowed* to cool, and readings of the temperature *were taken* every minute.
6   The water *was stirred* continually throughout the experiment.
7   The value of the temperature *was noted* at every reading.
8   The experiment *was continued* until the temperature of the water was well below 0°C.
9   The water *was observed* carefully as the temperature approached 0°C.
10   The stirring was continued and the temperature *was noted* for several minutes after ice formed in the calorimeter.
11   A graph of temperature against time *was plotted* from the tabulation of the results.

12   From the graph and the observations which *were made* during the
experiment, deductions *were made* as to what takes place when the
temperature of water is lowered.

C This part introduces the question form of the past simple passive. The
table should be used to ask questions about the report of the experiment
which has just been completed by the students. Students should ask and
answer these questions in pairs.

D The question form *why*+past simple passive is introduced. Questions in
this form, which enquire about the reason why something was or was not
done, may be answered by statements beginning with *In order to, In order
not to, So as to, So as not to.*
    Students are asked to make questions and answer them, using the two
tables provided.

E The following set of results should be dictated to the class, who write
them into a table.

time (mins)	temperature (°C)
0	58
1	31
2	18
3	9
4	3·5
5	0
6	−2·5
7	0
8	0
9	0
10	0
11	0

    When these values have been noted, the students should plot the graph
of the results of the experiment.
    Students should compare their completed graphs to ensure that the
values have been understood correctly. The graph should be in this shape:

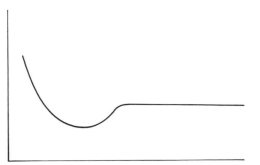

SECTION 2 **reporting observations and results; stating
conclusions**

A The text should be studied by the class, and exploited by the teacher in
the various ways outlined for text study in the previous units. A series of
comprehension questions are given in the Student's Book. These may be
used for oral or written work, and may be supplemented by further
questions if desired. Particular attention should be paid to the way in
which a **conclusion** is drawn at the end of the passage:

It can be stated that ...
Heat energy must therefore have been absorbed ...
It can therefore be concluded that ...

B The construction

The temperature continued to fall for a short time **without any ice
forming.** is introduced, taking this example from the passage in **A**. The
meaning of the sentence with this construction is explained as being the
same as the sentence *The temperature continued to fall for a short time,
but no ice formed.* The second example should also be studied, and further
examples given if necessary before the exercise in the formation of this
structure is attempted.

1   A metal wire was stretched 5 cm without breaking.
2   Mercury was cooled to −20°C without freezing.
3   Sand was added to water and the mixture was heated gently for a
    long time without the sand dissolving.
4   Some aluminium was placed in water and left for some time without
    any reaction being observed.
5   A current was passed through a wire for a period of time without any
    heating effect being detected.
6   A substance was heated for a short time without any rise in
    temperature being observed.
7   Various substances were placed in dilute hydrochloric acid, without
    any gas being evolved.
8   Some ammonium chloride was heated without any ammonia being
    smelt.
9   A lighted splint was held over the top of a test-tube of gas without
    any explosion being heard.
10 A suspended magnet was brought near to a coil of wire without any
    effect on the magnet being noticed.

C Here, the verbs commonly used when **reporting results and observations**
are grouped together. The use of *could be* in addition to *was* and *were*
with the past passive is introduced, as in *bubbles of gas could be seen.*
Students should make statements from the table, imagining they are
reporting an experiment they have carried out. Some words in the table
may need to be explained. For example,

effervescence	a stream of small bubbles
decrepitation	a crackling sound made when water is driven off from crystals
popping	noise
pungent	very strong (used with smells)

D The expression of **deduction** is introduced, using the construction *must be* as in *This must be due to a reaction taking place*. When deductions are being made about results which were observed in the past, the construction *must have been* is used: *This must have been due to a reaction*. Similar statements may be made from the table. Students should first make statements about what happened during an experiment. For example,

During the experiment, bubbles of gas could be observed.

They should then follow these statements with deductions as to the reason for this observed phenomenon:

This must have been due to carbon dioxide being given off.

Students will have to choose the wording of their first statements for themselves, but they should be based on the work covered in **C**.

E The sequence of **procedure, observation, deduction** and **reason** is identified, and an example is set out showing how this sequence can be incorporated into a text. The example should be studied carefully.

Similar statements may be made with the notes in this exercise, although the exact phrasing may of course vary, together with the particular words chosen by individual students. Suitable answers are given here, but they are not the only correct versions.

1   An electric current was passed through a coil of wire. A heating effect was detected. This must have been due to the current passing through the wire, because no other source of energy was available.

2   Pieces of marble were placed in dilute acid. Bubbles of gas were observed. This must have been caused by carbon dioxide being evolved, since the gas turned lime water cloudy.

3   Hydrogen peroxide was placed in a test-tube with manganese dioxide. An effervescence was observed. This must have been caused by hydrogen being liberated, since the gas caused a glowing splint to ignite.

4   Copper sulphate crystals were heated in a test-tube. A decrepitation was noticed. This must have been because of water in the crystals expanding due to the heat given to the crystals.

5   Some chemicals were heated in a test-tube. A popping sound was heard. This must have been due to bubbles of gas exploding, since bubbles of gas were observed during the experiment.

6   Slaked lime and ammonium chloride were heated. A pungent smell was detected. This must have been caused by ammonia being evolved, because the gas caused damp red litmus paper to turn blue.

SECTION 3   **describing and accounting for results**

A This exercise may be treated as a class exercise, the whole class or individual students being asked to complete the text with suitable forms of the verbs. The text describes the procedure and results of a simple experiment to demonstrate the phenomenon of osmosis. The complete text should read as follows:

Two beakers *were filled* with water. In each beaker a glass cylinder *was immersed*, across the bottom of which a membrane *was tied*. The membrane *allowed* water to pass through it freely, but it would not allow molecules of dissolved protein to pass through it, since protein molecules *are* larger than molecules of water. A membrane which *allows* molecules to pass through it *is known as* a permeable membrane. However, since the membranes used in this experiment *allowed* only molecules of a liquid to pass through, they *are known as* semi-permeable membranes.

Two protein solutions *were* then *made up*, one at a concentration of $5 \, g \, dm^{-3}$, and the other at $10 \, g \, dm^{-3}$. Some of the $5 \, g \, dm^{-3}$ solution *was poured* into one of the glass cylinders, and some of the $10 \, g \, dm^{-3}$ solution into the other cylinder.

The level of the water in the beakers and the protein solution in the glass cylinders *were adjusted* until they *were* all equal. The experiment *was* then *left* for a period of twenty four hours.

After twenty-four hours, it *was observed* that the levels of the water and protein solutions *were* considerably different from when the experiment *was begun*. The level of liquid in the cylinders *was seen* to be higher than the level of the water in the beakers. Moreover, when the height of the liquid in each cylinder *was measured*, it *was found* that the height of the column of liquid in the cylinder containing the more concentrated solution *was* twice the height of that containing the other solution.

When the text has been completed and new words and expressions have been explained, the teacher may ask simple comprehension questions to establish that the text has been generally understood. The questions in **B** are more formal comprehension questions, the answers to which may be written up together by the class, or by students individually.

B Suitable model answers are:

1   A semi-permeable membrane will allow only some molecules of liquid to pass through it.
2   Protein solution.
3   One solution was twice as concentrated as the other.
4   The levels of the water in the beakers and the protein solution in the glass cylinders were adjusted until they were all equal.
5   24 hours.
6   The levels of the water and protein solutions were considerably different from when the experiment was begun.
7   The height of the liquid in each cylinder.

8   The height of the column of liquid in the cylinder containing the more concentrated solution was twice the height of that containing the other solution.

    Students' answers to Questions 9 and 10 will clearly differ, and should be based on class discussion of the results and students' attempts to account for the results described.

 C This text gives an explanation of the results of the osmosis experiment. It may be treated in the way outlined in previous units for the exploitation of a text. Attention should be drawn to the way in which conclusions are drawn from the observations, using expressions such as *it seems that* and *this means that*. Students should compare their own explanation of the results of the experiment with the one printed here. Differences and disagreements as to the cause of the results may be discussed.

D Questions and statements involving *seems* and *appears* are set out. These may be practised with information based on the text, before the next exercise is attempted. The expression *it looks as if* may also be mentioned, drawing attention to the fact that it is a less formal expression, and so it is not practised here. Suitable model answers for these questions are:

1   Because the membranes used were semi-permeable, and would not allow protein molecules to pass through them.
2   It seems that the membrane must be capable of supporting a certain pressure of solution and preventing the solution from passing through it.
3   X cm. (The more concentrated solution exerts twice as much pressure as the less concentrated solution.)
4   The solutions would flow into the beakers until the levels of liquid inside and outside the cylinders were equal.
5   It appears that there was a driving force.
6   No. It appears that when the column of solution reached a certain height, the passage of water molecules through the membrane stopped.
7   The pressure of solution on the membrane, the driving force which causes the water molecules to move across the membrane, and atmospheric pressure.
8   It seems that the pressure acting on the membrane from the column of solution and the driving force causing molecules to pass through the membrane became equal, and equilibrium was obtained.

E The passage setting out the conclusion to the experiment should then be studied in detail.

F Questions involving speculation as to possible results are introduced. These are introduced by *supposing* and *what would have happened if*, followed by the past perfect. *Instead of* is also introduced here. These questions and the statements used for their answers are of the kind encountered in type 3 conditional questions and statements.

    No key is given for this exercise, as the questions and answers are likely

116

unit 9
classwork
section 3

to vary considerably with individual students. The exercise should be
treated as a class exercise, with students asking and answering questions
in pairs. The whole class may decide whether particular answers are
acceptable statements of what would have happened.

exercises

exercise 1

Some ammonium chloride was placed in a test-tube and some sodium hydroxide was added. The test-tube was held over a low bunsen burner flame and the contents were heated gently for a time. The test-tube was moved from side to side in the flame in order to ensure a gentle heating action. The reaction which took place was observed carefully. A piece of dry red litmus paper was held over the mouth of the test-tube and the result was observed. The litmus paper was moistened and again held over the mouth of the test-tube. The result was again observed. Care was taken not to inhale a lot of the gas, but the gas given off during the reaction was carefully smelt.

exercise 2

1   As the mixture in the test-tube was heated, a reaction could be detected due to bubbles of gas which appeared in the liquid.
2   When a piece of dry red litmus paper was held over the mouth of the test-tube, no change in colour was observed even though it was held there for some time.
3   However, when the litmus paper was moistened, it turned blue when held over the mouth of the test-tube.
4   This must have been due to an alkaline gas being given off during the reaction.
5   When the gas was smelt carefully, it was found to have a very strong smell.
6   This must have been ammonia, since the smell was unmistakable.
7   It can therefore be concluded that during the experiment, ammonia was given off as a result of a reaction between ammonium chloride and sodium hydroxide.

exercise 3   The following are model answers; differences in wording are possible.

1   No osmotic pressure would have been set up.
2   No osmotic pressure would have been set up.
3   Water would have passed through the membrane from the solution in the beaker into the solution in the cylinder.
4   Water would have passed through the membrane from the solution in the cylinder into the solution in the beaker.
5   A greater osmotic pressure would have been set up.
6   The osmotic pressure would have been smaller.
7   The solutions would have been osmotically balanced on either side of the membrane. (No rise in level of the solution in the cylinder would have occurred.)
8   Osmotic pressure would have caused water from the less concentrated solution to pass through the membrane into the more concentrated solution.

drills

drill 1

1 What did you do first?
I crushed some ice and mixed it with salt.
First some ice was crushed and mixed with salt.

2 Then what did you do?
I placed the mixture in a large container.
Then the mixture was placed in a large container.

3 What did you do next?
I poured a small amount of hot water into a calorimeter.
Next a small amount of hot water was poured into a calorimeter.

4 What did you do with the calorimeter?
I inserted it into the freezing mixture.
The calorimeter was inserted into the freezing mixture.

5 What did you do after that?
I allowed the water to cool.
After that the water was allowed to cool.

6 What did you do while the water was cooling?
I took readings of the temperature at one minute intervals.
While the water was cooling, readings of the temperature were taken at one minute intervals.

7 What else did you do throughout the experiment?
I stirred the water.
Throughout the experiment the water was stirred.

8 How long did you continue the experiment?
Until the temperature of the water was well below 0°C.
The experiment was continued until the temperature of the water was well below 0°C.

9 What did you do as the temperature approached 0°C?
I observed the water carefully.
As the temperature approached 0°C, the water was observed carefully.

10 What did you do from the results?
I plotted a graph.
From the results a graph was plotted.

drill 2

1 The liquid was heated. When the temperature reached 100°C, the heating was stopped.
The liquid was heated until the temperature reached 100°C.

2 The material was stretched. When it was 50 cm long, the stretching was stopped.
The material was stretched until it was 50 cm long.

3 The current was increased. When it rose to 200 amps it was kept constant.
The current was increased until it rose to 200 amps.

4 The solution was stirred. When all the solid dissolved, the stirring was stopped.
The solution was stirred until all the solid dissolved.

5 The solution was heated. When all the liquid evaporated, the heating was stopped.
The solution was heated until all the liquid evaporated.

6 The gas was pressurized. When it became liquid the pressure was kept constant.
The gas was pressurized until it became liquid.

7 Acid was added to the solution. When the indicator changed colour, no more acid was added.
Acid was added to the solution until the indicator changed colour.

8 The voltage was increased. When the voltmeter indicated 1,000 volts, the voltage was kept constant.
The voltage was increased until the voltmeter indicated 1,000 volts.

9 The temperature was lowered. When the water froze, the temperature was kept constant.
The temperature was lowered until the water froze.

10 The solution in the test-tube was heated. When a pungent smell was detected, the heating was stopped.
The solution in the test-tube was heated until a pungent smell was detected.

drill 3 Students should be introduced to words describing sounds and to the distinction between *throughout* and *from time to time* before starting this drill.

1 When the experiment was carried out, this sound was heard all the time—(*Sound*)
Throughout the experiment a crackling sound was heard.

2 Sometimes, this sound was noticed—(*Sound*)
From time to time during the experiment a popping sound was noticed.

3 Occasionally, this sound was heard—(*Sound*)
From time to time during the experiment a howling sound was heard.

4 While the experiment was being carried out, this sound was constantly noticed—(*Sound*)
Throughout the experiment a whistling sound was noticed.

5 Sometimes, this sound was noticed—(*Sound*)
From time to time during the experiment a rattling sound was noticed.

6 All the time the experiment was in progress, this sound could be heard—(*Sound*)
Throughout the experiment a scraping sound could be heard.

7 Occasionally, this sound was noticed—(*Sound*)
From time to time during the experiment a squeaking sound was noticed.

8 While the experiment was being conducted, this sound was heard all the time—(*Sound*)
Throughout the experiment a hissing sound was heard.

9 At times, this sound was heard during the experiment—(*Sound*)
From time to time during the experiment a banging sound was heard.

10 At the end of the experiment this sound was heard—(*Sound*)
At the end of the experiment an explosion was heard.

drill 4

1 There was a terrible smell during the experiment. Do you think it was
due to carbon dioxide or hydrogen sulphide?
*It can't have been due to carbon dioxide—it must have been due to
hydrogen sulphide.*

2 There was an explosion during the experiment. Do you suppose it was
caused by oxygen or hydrogen?
*It can't have been caused by oxygen—it must have been caused by
hydrogen.*

3 Heat was given off during the experiment. Do you think this was due
to an electrical effect or a chemical effect?
*It can't have been due to an electrical effect—it must have been due
to a chemical effect.*

4 During the experiment, damp red litmus paper turned blue. Do you
think this was caused by an acidic gas or an alkaline gas?
*It can't have been caused by an acidic gas—it must have been caused
by an alkaline gas.*

5 After the experiment, the wire was longer than at the beginning. Do
you think this was caused by a compressive force or a tensile force?
*It can't have been caused by a compressive force—it must have been
caused by a tensile force.*

6 When a magnetic pole was brought near the north pole of a
suspended magnet, the poles repelled each other. Was the magnetic
pole a south pole or a north pole?
It can't have been a south pole—it must have been a north pole.

7 An unknown powder was added to water in a beaker. When the
powder was stirred, it dissolved. Do you think it was sand or salt?
It can't have been sand—it must have been salt.

8 A metal was left in water for several months. It did not corrode. Do
you think it was iron or aluminium?
It can't have been iron—it must have been aluminium.

drill 5

1 What appears to have caused water to rise up the cylinder?
It appears that a force caused it to rise up the cylinder.

2 What seems to have prevented the solution mixing with the water?
It seems that the membrane prevented them mixing.

3 What seems to have happened to the water level in the beaker during
the experiment?
It seems that it fell.

4 What appears to have happened to the level of liquid in the cylinder
during the experiment?
It appears that it rose.

5 What appears to have happened to the $10 \, g \, dm^{-3}$ solution?
It appears that it rose more than the $5 \, g \, dm^{-3}$ solution.

6   What seems to have happened when the pressure of liquid on the membrane reached a certain point?
It seems that it prevented further movement of water into the cylinder.

7   What seems to have happened to the osmotic force and the force on the membrane at a certain point?
It seems that they became equal.

8   What appears to have happened when these forces became equal?
It appears that no more water passed into the cylinder.

drill 6

1   What would have happened to the results if glucose had been used instead of protein?
The results would have been similar.

2   What would have happened to the liquid in the cylinder if an impermeable membrane had been used?
The liquid in the cylinder would not have risen.

3   What would have happened to the column of liquid if a solution four times as concentrated had been used?
The column of liquid would have been four times as high.

4   What would have happened to the solution in the cylinder if a protein solution of equal concentration had been placed in the beaker?
The solution in the cylinder would not have risen.

5   What would have happened to the column of liquid in the cylinder if the membrane had been punctured?
The column of liquid would have fallen.

6   What would have happened to the water and the protein solution if a fully-permeable membrane had been used?
The water and the protein solution would have mixed.

7   What would have happened to the level of liquid in the cylinder if a mixture of sand and water had been placed in the cylinder?
The level of liquid in the cylinder would have remained the same.

8   What would have happened to the liquid in the cylinder if water had been used in both the cylinder and the beaker?
The liquid in the cylinder would not have risen.

activity

The graph should be used as the basis for speculating and concluding what took place during the experiment in which naphthalene (the substance from which moth-balls are made) was first melted and then allowed to cool while measurements of the temperature were made at regular intervals.

If possible, the graph should be copied onto the board, or made into an overhead projection transparency, so that the class can all see it at the same time and can discuss what they think happened at various points on the graph. This will involve making statements and asking questions with the structures used for speculating and concluding which have been introduced in this unit. These should include:

probably	must be	must have	must have been due to
			must have been caused by
seems to have	appears to have	it seems that	it looks as if
it appears that	this means that	therefore	thus
because	since	in order to	so as to

Students may be asked questions about the graph by the teacher, or they may ask each other questions in pairs. The class as a whole can then discuss whether the explanations and conclusions put forward are likely to be correct.

If desired, the class may construct a conclusion to the experiment together, the teacher writing this on the board. This may be similar to the following model:

When the substance was heated and allowed to cool, the temperature did not increase or decrease regularly with time. Both the heating and cooling curves show that during heating and cooling there were periods of time when the naphthalene did not increase or decrease in temperature. However, during these periods heat continued to be either gained or lost, since the naphthalene was first heated and then cooled regularly.

Heat is a form of energy. During the experiment, energy in the form of heat was required to bring about a rise in temperature when the naphthalene was heated. This energy was then given off in the form of heat when the naphthalene was allowed to cool. However, the heating and cooling curves show that the temperature rise and fall was not uniform, although heat energy was imparted and lost continually during the heating and cooling stages respectively. This means that for a period of time during the heating stage, energy seems to have been required continually, even though the temperature did not rise all the time. During the cooling stage, the heat energy given off did not result in a loss in temperature for one period of time. This again indicates that energy was required for another purpose.

During the experiment, the solid first liquefied when heated, and then solidified when cooled. The substance underwent two changes of state. If the results are considered, it is seen that at the points where the changes of state took place, no change in temperature was apparent. It therefore appears that heat energy must have been absorbed by the naphthalene at certain times when being heated and cooled in order to bring about a change of state.

From the results of this experiment, it can be concluded (inferred) that energy is required in order to bring about a change of state in a substance.

unit 10

classwork

SECTION 1 **describing an experiment**

This section deals with describing experiments, and therefore involves a variety of tenses; in particular the future tenses. The language used should be distinguished from reporting experiments, as found in the previous unit.

It would assist the presentation in this section if the demonstration described in **A** could actually be carried out in the classroom. It requires two transparent containers of water, and quantities of sand and sugar. Students are asked to describe what takes place as the demonstration progresses. The terms *solution* and *suspension* may be elicited from the students if they are already known, or presented if they have not been met before.

 A The text is studied in the usual manner, and new words and expressions are introduced. If the demonstration has been carried out in the classroom, the contents of the containers may be examined to see if they actually correspond to the description in this passage. Particular attention should be paid to the use in the passage of the future tense, and to expressions such as: *no matter how*, *even if*, *on the other hand*, *despite* and *have failed to*.

The passage for completion should be treated as a class exercise. It should be completed as follows:

Take some salt and stir it into some water in a beaker. It *will dissolve* readily. Now do the same with some chalk. Very little *will dissolve*. It *will be observed* that chalk is less soluble than salt: chalk can be said to be relatively insoluble.

Continue to add salt to the salt solution, stirring continually. A point *will be reached* where the salt fails to dissolve. When no more salt *will dissolve* in the water, the solution is said to be saturated. It *will be noticed* that adding more salt *will result in* the salt being deposited as a sediment at the bottom of the beaker.

Consider what *will happen* if a saturated solution is boiled. As the solution is heated, more salt *will dissolve* until the boiling point is reached and the solution is again saturated. Boiling *will cause* the water to evaporate, and the volume of water *will therefore be reduced*. The salt, however, *will remain* in the solution, so that the same amount of salt *will be present* in a smaller volume of water. The smaller volume of water *will not be able* to hold all the salt in solution, so salt *will begin* to appear as a solid. When a substance is deposited as a solid while a solution is being heated, it is said to crystallize out.

B The expressions *despite* and *in spite of* should be introduced, using the examples in the Student's Book and other examples which the teacher may supply. The use of *fail to* should be explained, again with suitable examples if necessary.

1 In spite of/Despite being heated to a high temperature, the solid fails to melt.
2 In spite of/Despite being heated together, the two chemicals fail to react.

3   In spite of/Despite being cooled to a very low temperature, the gas fails to liquefy.

4   In spite of/Despite being cooled to 0°C, the liquid fails to freeze.

5   In spite of/Despite being compressed to a very high pressure, the gas fails to explode.

6   In spite of/Despite being brought near to some metal objects, the magnet fails to attract them.

7   In spite of/Despite having a high current passed along it, the wire fails to melt.

8   In spite of/Despite being connected to an electric cell, the lamp fails to light.

C The words *keep*, *remain*, *leave* and *continue* should be identified and distinguished. The examples in the book may be supplemented if necessary.

1   The solid was heated to a high temperature, but it *remained* solid and did not liquefy.

2   The temperature of the substance was *kept* constant for a length of time.

3   Heating was *continued* until the metal changed colour.

4   The solution was *left* for a long period of time without any effect being noticed.

5   When the mixture reached a certain temperature, it was *left* to cool slowly.

6   When the solution was heated, all the water evaporated but solid crystals *were left/remained* in the bottom of the dish.

7   When the temperature of the liquid reached 0°C, cooling was *continued* for some time until a change of state took place.

8   The temperature of the liquid was *kept* at boiling point for as long as possible so that all the liquid evaporated.

9   The substance was allowed to *remain* in the acid until it began to react.

10 When salt began to dissolve in the water, the experiment was *continued* until the solution became saturated.

11 During the experiment, the current through the coil was *kept* as low as possible.

12 After being stirred, the suspension was *left* until all the solid particles settled at the bottom of the beaker.

D The use of the prefixes *in-*, *im-*, and *un-* should be introduced by means of the examples. The words given should then be arranged in columns in the following way:

in-	**im-**	**un-**
invalid	impossible	unlikely
inexact	impure	uncertain
incorrect	imperfect	untrue
invisible	impractical	unequal

in-	im-	un-
inappropriate	implausible	unusual
indirect		uncommon
inactive		unsuitable
inconvenient		unusable
inaccurate		unable
incomplete		unstable
insignificant		unreasonable
insufficient		unknown
		uneven
		unsatisfactory
		unfavourable
		unmistakable
		uncontaminated
		unidentified

SECTION 2 stating results

This section deals with the present perfect tense used to describe recent action or result, and a variety of tenses used in describing experimental procedure.

It would help the presentation in **A** if two transparent containers containing a solution of salt and water and a suspension of sand and water could be presented to the class. The activity in **A** would then be centred around the actual containers rather than the diagrams. The presentation can make use of the diagrams only if necessary.

If it is possible to actually add salt to one container of liquid and sand to the other during the course of the lesson and observe the results, this would lead to a more realistic presentation of the present perfect tense when questions such as *What has happened to the solid in beaker A?* are asked. The tense would then be used in an appropriate context to describe recent action.

A The answers to the questions relating to the diagrams or to the presentation should be similar to the following:

1　The solid in beaker A has disappeared, whereas the solid in beaker B is still present.
2　(a) The salt has dissolved.
　　(b) The sand has not dissolved.
3　The liquid in beaker A is a solution, whereas the liquid in beaker B is a suspension.

B Students are asked to imagine that an experiment is being carried out, and that the results are being reported soon after they have occurred. The table is used to produce six sentences using the present perfect in this context.

The sentences, when complete, refer to an experiment in which carbon dioxide has been produced. The present perfect passive is therefore introduced with the example *Carbon dioxide has been produced*.

C This exercise may be completed by the class together. It consists of a series of situations which describe recent action and result, using the present perfect active and passive. The wording of the class statements may vary from the following examples:

1 Red litmus paper has been dampened and held over the test-tube. The litmus has turned blue, therefore ammonia has been given off during the experiment.
2 A current has been passed through a wire. The wire has become hot, therefore a heating effect has been produced.
3 Two powdered solids have been stirred into a liquid. The solids have dissolved completely, therefore a solution has been formed.
4 A gas has been produced as a result of a reaction. The gas has caused a glowing splint to catch fire, therefore oxygen has been given off.
5 A solution has been left in a cylinder, separated from a beaker of water by a membrane. The solution has risen up the cylinder, therefore a force has caused the water to pass through the membrane.
6 A tensile force has been applied to a wire. The wire has become permanently stretched, therefore the elastic limit has been exceeded.
7 A metal block has been heated. The block has become larger, therefore expansion has taken place.
8 A magnet has been suspended freely. A second magnet has caused the suspended magnet to swing away from it, therefore repulsion has taken place.

D It would be an advantage if the actions could actually be performed by the teacher on real objects in front of the class, so that statements are made in realistic contexts. The class should then make statements saying what has been done to the objects in the illustrations:

1 It's been stretched. (*Example*)
2 It's been twisted.
3 It's been cracked.
4 It's been torn/ripped.
5 It's been snapped/broken/fractured.
6 It's been folded.
7 It's been shattered/broken.
8 It's been scratched.

E The passage makes use of a variety of tenses in order to give instructions, and state what will happen when the experiment is carried out. The class should study the passage with the teacher, and discuss the answers to the questions which are interposed in the text. The questions should lead to a short discussion of the part of the text studied, before a statement is made which answers a particular question. Suitable answers would state:

1 The solution has become saturated.
2 No more copper sulphate crystals will dissolve because the solution is saturated.

3   The solid crystals left in the solution will settle in the beaker.
4   It has demonstrated that more copper sulphate is soluble at a higher temperature.
5   As the solution cools, the copper sulphate becomes less soluble.
6   There will be a quantity of solid crystals and the solution will be saturated.

F The passage may be completed by the students together, using a variety of tenses.

Add a moderate quantity of salt to a beaker of water and stir the mixture vigorously until all the salt *has dissolved*. Continue to add salt, still stirring the solution, until no more *will dissolve* and a deposit of salt *is observed* in the bottom of the beaker. Heat the solution (which is now saturated) gently. It *will be noticed* that the excess salt begins to dissolve. Continue heating gently until all the salt *has dissolved*. Consider what *has been demonstrated* by this procedure. Now transfer the solution to an evaporating dish and heat it more strongly until it *boils*. After a while it *will be observed* that the liquid level *is reduced* as the water *evaporates*, but at the same time salt *begins/will begin* to appear in solid form. Consider what *has caused* salt to appear as the water evaporates. Continue to boil the solution until all the water *has evaporated*.

The class should now be able to give an account of what will cause solid salt to appear when a saturated solution of salt is boiled. In outline, what will happen is that water will be lost due to evaporation as it is boiled. Since there is less water in which the salt can dissolve, the solution becomes less able to contain all of the salt, and solid salt begins to crystallize out of the solution. More salt crystallizes out as more water evaporates, until all the water has evaporated and only solid salt is left.

SECTION 3   **describing and accounting for a phenomenon**

Surface tension may be demonstrated very simply by means of some soap solution (liquid detergent may be used, such as washing-up liquid) and a wire ring. These are often sold for children to play with, but can be easily made by the teacher if necessary. When the ring is dipped into the soap solution and air is blown against the film of soap solution across the ring, soap bubbles may be formed which finally float free of the ring and around the room. If it is possible to present such a demonstration in class, students may be asked to construct their own account of the stages involved in the formation of soap bubbles. This could be done before the students look at the account, the teacher guiding the account along the lines on that page, and writing up a final version. This can later be compared to the account in the book.

   If it is not possible to conduct this presentation, the account in the book may be studied with reference to the diagrams only.

A In studying this text, as well as introducing new expressions and inserting comprehension checks in the usual way, the teacher should draw attention to various features such as the variety of tenses used, the connectors used (*as*, *since*, etc), and the use of *obviously* and *clearly*. After reading and studying the text, students should be familiar with the basic concept of surface tension, which is developed further in this section.

The questions are designed primarily as prompts for oral work in the classroom, and answers will obviously differ from individual students. No key is therefore given here. The questions may be used as the basis for written answers from the students after the initial oral exercise.

Facts the teacher may need in these questions are:

8   Soap film is not unique in exhibiting this phenomenon. All liquids display surface tension effects.

9   It is possible to measure the quantity of the surface tension force in different liquids, by experimental means. An example of such an experiment is given below.

10. Soap is used to demonstrate surface tension effects because it shows these effects quite clearly, and these effects are fairly familiar from everyday experience. Bubbles could not have been formed with pure water only, since the surface tension of water would not have been suitable.

B The remainder of this section is devoted to exercises based on a description of an experimental method of measuring surface tension. The experimental procedure and the apparatus used is described in some detail. However, neither the students nor the teacher should be over-concerned with the problems and details of this particular experiment. It should serve as an example of how experimental procedure is often set out in textbooks. Students should be able to understand the construction of the apparatus and the method used, but a detailed understanding of the theory and the way in which the equations are arrived at is not necessary. The concern here should be with the language of the text rather than the detailed scientific content.

Students are asked to write a description of the apparatus using the diagram and the notes provided. A minimum of guidance is given in the book, and so it is for the teacher to decide if the class will need more guidance and if the exercise therefore needs to be completed by the class working together. More confident groups of students may be left to draw up the description on their own.

The sections on aim, theory and method may then be studied by the class and the teacher in the same way as previous texts in the course. Attention should be given to features such as tenses and connectors, as well as to new vocabulary and expressions. It is not necessary for the class to understand the details of the theory or how the mathematical formulae are arrived at.

C The questions in this section are intended to be answered by the class working together, but they may be used for written work as follow-up to the classwork.

The facts which should be included in students' answers are set out below:

2 (a) A column of liquid will be drawn up.
   (b) A complex form of cylinder.
   (c) To account for the complex shape which the column of liquid takes in reality.

3 (a) By examining it in relation to its reflection in the water as it is lowered towards the surface of the liquid.
   (b) By soaking them in chromic acid.
   (c) So that they are wetted completely by the water.
   (d) The level of the arm should be raised so that the ring is about 0·5 cm below the surface of the water.
   (e) The beam is returned to the horizontal by lowering the platform.
   (f) The column of liquid suspended from the ring will break, and the beam will jump upwards.

4 (a) At 'standard' atmospheric pressure, pure water boils when the temperature *reaches* 100°C.
   (b) The north pole of a suspended magnet will be repelled as another north pole *approaches* it.
   (c) Crystals began to appear in the liquid when the saturation point was *reached*.
   (d) The liquid was not allowed to freeze, but observations were made as the freezing point was *approached*.
   (e) As the melting point was *approached*, the solid began to change colour before it actually liquefied.

exercises

exercise 1

1   When carrying out any experiment involving chemicals it is important to ensure that the chemicals used are *uncontaminated*. Chemicals which are *impure* may be *unstable* or *inactive*, so that they are in fact *unusable*. If the experimenter is *unable* to use fresh, pure chemicals, he may find that it is *impossible* to perform the experiment, or that the results are *unsatisfactory*.

2   In any experiment, the accuracy with which measurements are made is vital. *Inaccurate* or *incomplete* measurements are likely to make the whole experiment *invalid*, since *inexact* measurements are *unlikely* to produce a satisfactory set of results.

3   Sometimes during an experiment an *unknown* gas is given off. If the experimenter is *uncertain* about the nature of a gas he should be extremely careful when testing it. However, it is *unusual* for a gas such as hydrogen sulphide or ammonia to be *unidentified*, as the smell of these gases is *unmistakable*.

exercise 2

Place some naphthalene in a test-tube and allow the tube to remain in a container of boiling water until all of the solid *has melted*. When all of the naphthalene *has liquefied*, allow it to cool, stirring it continually and taking regular measurements of the temperature. As it cools, the naphthalene *will solidify*. When it *has completely solidified*, the thermometer *will be* 'stuck' in the solid mass. It *will then be possible* to repeat the experiment, taking measurements of temperature while the naphthalene is being heated in order to obtain similar results for the melting of the solid. When the results of the experiment for both melting and solidifying *have been plotted* on a graph, the cooling and melting curves *will both be shown*. It *will be apparent* from the curves that energy *has been required* for the melting and cooling stages.

exercise 3

1   The ring has been dipped in soap solution. A film of soap has formed across the ring.

2   Air has been blown gently onto the surface of the film. The film has stretched into a rounded shape due to the pressure of the air.

3   More air has been blown into the film. The film has stretched further and has taken on a bulbous shape. It has not yet separated itself from the ring.

4   The film has sealed itself into a sphere. It has completely enclosed the air inside and has floated away from the wire ring.

5   The surface tension in the film has allowed it to stretch. It has then enclosed the air within it and has formed a bubble.

drills

drill 1

1 Will the solid remain in suspension even if it is stirred vigorously?
Yes, it will remain in suspension no matter how vigorously it is stirred.

2 Will the substance remain in solution even if it is left standing for a long time?
Yes, it will remain in solution no matter how long it is left standing.

3 Will the material remain solid even if it is heated strongly?
Yes, it will remain solid no matter how strongly it is heated.

4 Will the solid remain in suspension even if it is heated strongly?
Yes, it will remain in suspension no matter how strongly it is heated.

5 Will the container withstand shock even if it is hit violently?
Yes, it will withstand shock no matter how violently it is hit.

6 Will the material continue to extend if the tensile force is very great?
Yes, it will continue to extend no matter how great the tensile force is.

7 Will the substances react even if the temperature is very low?
Yes, they will react no matter how low the temperature is.

8 Will sand fail to dissolve in water even if the temperature is high?
Yes, it will fail to dissolve in water no matter how high the temperature is.

drill 2

1 Did the water remain liquid even though heat was lost?
Yes, it remained liquid despite the loss of heat.

2 Did the temperature continue to rise even though there was a lack of heat?
Yes, it continued to rise despite the lack of heat.

3 Was the pressure kept constant even though there was a decrease in volume?
Yes, it was kept constant despite the decrease in volume.

4 Did the solid remain in suspension even though there was vigorous stirring?
Yes, it remained in suspension despite the vigorous stirring.

5 Was the liquid left in the container even though there was a danger of contamination?
Yes, it was left in the container despite the danger of contamination.

6 Was the temperature kept low even though there was a risk of freezing?
Yes, it was kept low despite the risk of freezing.

7 Did the concentration remain high even though water was added?
Yes, it remained high despite the addition of water.

8 Was the container left to cool even though there was a risk of it cracking?
Yes, it was left to cool despite the risk of it cracking.

9 Did the temperature remain constant even though there was an increase in heat?
Yes, it remained constant despite the increase in heat.

10 Was the experiment continued even though there was a risk of explosion?
Yes, it was continued despite the risk of explosion.

drill 3

1 How do you know that carbon dioxide is present?
Because the lime water has turned cloudy.

2 How can you be sure that ammonia has been produced?
Because damp red litmus paper has turned blue.

3 How do you know that the steel is at a temperature of 300°C?
Because the colour of the metal has turned blue.

4 How do you know that the freezing-point of the liquid has been reached?
Because the liquid has turned solid.

5 How do you know that the two solids have reached their melting points?
Because both solids have turned liquid.

6 How do you know that water has been absorbed by the crystals?
Because the white crystals have turned blue.

7 How do you know that an acidic solution has been formed?
Because the blue litmus paper has turned red.

8 How do you know that radiation has been given off?
Because photographic paper has turned black.

drill 4

1 Has all of the solid dissolved in the liquid?
Yes, it has completely dissolved.

2 Have all of the results been collected?
Yes, they have all been collected.

3 Has all of the liquid solidified now?
Yes, it has completely solidified.

4 Have all of the chemical constituents been added to the mixture?
Yes, they have all been added.

5 Has all of the impurity been removed?
Yes, it has been completely removed.

6 Has all of the apparatus been re-assembled?
Yes, it has been completely re-assembled.

7 Have all of the batteries been tested?
Yes, they have all been tested.

8 Have all of the test-tubes been filled?
Yes, they have all been filled.

9 Have all of the samples been weighed?
Yes, they have all been weighed.

10 Has all of the naphthalene melted?
Yes, it has completely melted.

drill 5

1 Is it possible to manufacture gold from other metals?
No, it's quite impossible.

2 Is it likely these chemicals will react?
No, it's highly unlikely.

3 Are these results accurate?
No, they're extremely inaccurate.

4 Is this a very practical way of carrying out the experiment?
No, it's rather impractical.

5 Is this error in the results very significant?
No, it's fairly insignificant.

6 Is this a satisfactory way of tabulating the results?
No, it's quite unsatisfactory.

7 Is it usual for this to happen during the experiment?
No, it's very unusual.

8 Is uranium a common element?
No, it's extremely uncommon.

9 Is this an active substance before it's placed in the acid?
No, it's completely inactive.

10 Is this mixture quite stable?
No, it's highly unstable.

11 Is it known if there are smaller particles than the electron?
No, it's quite unknown.

12 Is it true that atomic energy is always very dangerous?
No, it's absolutely untrue.

drill 6

Part 1

1 Will the film of liquid form with any liquids?
No, it will only form if the liquid has a low surface tension.

2 Will the film distend on its own?
No, it will only distend if air is blown into it.

3 Will the film remain intact no matter how much air is blown into it?
No, it will only remain intact if air is blown into it gently.

4 Will the bubble be formed if no air is blown into the film?
No, it will only be formed if air is blown into it.

Part 2

1 Will the bubble continue to grow without air being blown into it?
No, it will only continue to grow as long as air is blown into it.

2 Will the film remain in the form of a bubble no matter what happens to it?
No, it will only remain in the form of a bubble as long as the film stays intact.

3 Will the molecules in the liquid film continue to move apart under normal conditions?

No, they will only continue to move apart as long as a force is applied to the film.

4   Will the bubble continue to exist under any conditions?
No, it will only continue to exist as long as the pressure inside is greater than the pressure outside.

activity

The class may require help from the teacher in interpreting the diagrams. Below is a summary of the information which should be included in the description of each stage of the four-stroke cycle. The words in italics are the names given to each stage of the cycle.

1 inlet valve open
  piston descending
  air and petrol mixture being drawn in (*induction*)

2 inlet valve closed
  piston begun to ascend
  air and petrol mixture being compressed (*compression*)

3 air and petrol mixture exploded by spark from spark plug
  piston begun to descend (forced downwards by force of explosion)
  both valves still closed (*power*)

4 exhaust valve open
  piston ascending
  piston begun to expel waste gas through exhaust valve (*exhaust*)
  camshaft and crankshaft rotate clockwise throughout

unit 11

classwork

SECTION 1   **understanding an explanation**

No new teaching points are presented in this unit. The unit is intended to draw together work which has already been covered in previous units. The object of the exercises in this unit is to provide the students with practice in understanding subject matter, using the language skills they have developed in the main body of the course.

The unit consists of a series of exercises in various forms. These exercises may be used in three different ways, depending on the purpose in mind:

1   As a series of class exercises, on which the students work together, discussing their answers and writing them up together, as in previous classwork sections.

2   As private study material, on which students work individually, and which the teacher then corrects or the class corrects together.

3   As test material. The teacher may set parts of the unit for the class to work on individually during lesson time. Students do not consult each other when writing up their answers. If all three classwork sections are set as test material, the lesson time will need to be extended accordingly, or the material set over a period of lessons.

Drills are provided in the usual way, and it is left to the teacher to decide whether to incorporate these into one of the three possible schemes outlined above. The drills consist of aural comprehension exercises as well as spoken drills, so that they may be incorporated into the scheme of a test situation if desired, to assess the students' oral/aural skills.

An Activity is also provided. You may wish to incorporate this into a form of assessment. This might be done by asking students individually to talk about the graphs provided. An assessment is then made of each student's oral/aural ability.

The teacher's notes to this unit consist largely of keys to the exercise material. Advice on handling the material is not given in such detail as in other units, since this will depend on the way in which you decide to treat this unit. Should you decide to cover the material in the style of previous units, the approaches outlined there for class study of texts, problem solving, answering comprehension questions and so on are easily adapted here.

It is quite possible to combine any of the possible approaches to the unit outlined above, treating some of the unit as test material, some as private study and some as classwork.

A

B

1	(c)	2	(a)	3	(b)	4	(c)	5	(a)
6	(b)	7	(c)	8	(c)	9	(a)	10	(c)

C The notes are used as the framework for either written or oral accounts of the constructions and function of the EFD generator. The exact wording of the description will obviously vary with the individual accounts.

D

E

1 (a) Turbulent flow is likely to occur.
  (b) Laminar flow is likely to continue.
2 (a) Turbulence is likely to occur.
  (b) Laminar flow is likely to continue.
3 Three: the pressure of the liquid, the diameter of the tube, the shape of the tube.
4 (a) and (c).
5 (b).
6 (a) It pushes the liquid forward through the water.
  (b) It is used in side-to-side movement in mixing with the water and striking the sides of the tube.

SECTION 2 describing apparatus and an experiment

A The following is a model answer only, as the wording and expressions used will obviously vary with individual students.

The apparatus used in the experiment consisted of a bulb containing air, a three-way tap, a pressure gauge, a beaker containing water, a thermometer and a stirrer. The bulb containing the air was connected to the pressure gauge by means of a small diameter tube, which was sealed into the bulb. The three-way tap was inserted at a point along the tube. The bulb was completely immersed in water which was contained in the beaker. The thermometer and the stirrer were placed in the water.

B The example below is a model answer only.

The apparatus was set up as described above. A flask with a large volume was used so as to minimize the effect of unheated air in the connecting tube and pressure gauge. The pressure indicated by the pressure gauge was noted. The temperature of the water was recorded. The water was heated. Readings of the temperature and pressure were taken at regular intervals throughout the experiment. The values of the temperature and the corresponding values of the pressure were recorded in a table. The water was stirred vigorously throughout the experiment. Since the temperature of the water could not be raised above 100°C, the experiment was stopped when the water boiled. A graph of pressure against temperature was plotted from the results.

C The following values should be read out by the teacher and taken down by the students so as to complete the table of results.

Pressure: nought point nine four
          nought point nine eight
          one point nought one

one point nought nine
one point one two
one point two three
one point two nine

Temperature: nought
          twelve
          twenty
          forty
          fifty
          eighty
          a hundred

The answers to the questions should be similar to the following model answers:

1   A straight-line graph.
2   It shows the relationship between the temperature and pressure of a gas.
3   They are directly proportional.
4   It can be stated that during the experiment, the gas expanded due to the heat energy.
5   It will pass through the point $-273°C$.
6   Zero.
7   If a gas were cooled to $-273°C$, the pressure of the gas would become zero.
8   Similar results would be obtained if a number of different gases were investigated. *Or:* Similar results would have been obtained if a number of different gases had been investigated.
9   The pressure of a fixed mass of gas at constant volume is directly proportional to its temperature. At $-273°C$, the pressure becomes zero.
10 The following formulae should be read out for the students to take down:

$p \propto x(t+273)$

(*p is directly proportional to t plus two hundred and seventy three, all in brackets, if t is the centigrade temperature.*)

$$\frac{t}{t+273} = \text{a constant value}$$

(*p over t plus two hundred and seventy three in brackets equals a constant value.*)

D

If a conductor is moved across a magnetic field, an electromotive force (e.m.f.) *will be produced* in the conductor. If the conductor *forms* part of a closed electrical circuit, the e.m.f. *will cause* an electric current to flow round the circuit. This effect *is known as* electromagnetic induction, and the e.m.f. *is said to be* 'induced' in the conductor as a result of its motion across the magnetic field.

If the following simple experiment *is carried out* the presence of an induced e.m.f. *will be demonstrated.* If the two ends of a coil of wire *are connected* to the terminals of a galvanometer, and a bar magnet *is brought* towards the coil, a deflection *will be observed* on the galvanometer. As the magnet *is moved* away from the coil, a deflection in the opposite direction *will be noticed*, no matter how near the magnet *is* to the coil.

Similarly, if the opposite pole of the magnet *is brought* towards the coil, the galvanometer deflection *will be* in the opposite direction. *It will be found* that the quicker the magnet *is moved* towards the coil, the greater the deflection *will be*.

If possible, the effects of using coils with different numbers of turns *should be investigated* as well as using magnets of different strengths.

SECTION 3   **giving instructions, interpreting results, describing attributes**

A The model below gives one possible way in which this exercise may be completed:

First the wire is attached to a fixed point. Next, a metre rule is positioned beside the wire. The position of the pointer on the rule should be noted. A weight is then added to the end of the wire. The position of the pointer on the rule is then noted again. More weights are added to the end of the wire, and the position of the pointer on the rule is noted each time. The values of the extension and load are then entered into the table. From the tabulated results a graph is plotted.

B
1 (b).   2 (a).   3 (b).   4 (a).   5 (b).

C
1 Glass is a *brittle transparent* solid which usually has a *smooth* surface. Although it is not usually very *strong*, it can be *toughened* in order to make it more *resilient*, so that it can be used, for instance, in car windscreens. However, in the liquid state, glass is extremely *ductile* and can be formed into almost any shape. It only becomes *brittle* when it *hardens*.

2 Copper is very ductile and malleable, and usually has a *shiny* yellow-orange appearance. Its *softness* allows it to be formed into a variety of shapes, often without the need to heat it. However, where *strength* is necessary, it is often alloyed with other metals such as cadmium in order to *strengthen* it.

3 Polythene is an extremely *resilient* material, and is often used where high *strength* combined with *flexibility* is required. It can be made either *transparent*, *translucent* or *opaque*, according to whether it is required to see through it; although usually very *strong*, it does become much *weaker* when heated, and will melt at relatively low temperatures.

4 Wood is a relatively *weak* substance, but its *strength* depends on its

thickness and variety. Some wood is extremely *pliable* when in the form of thin sheets, while other wood is extremely *hard* and *strong,* particularly when it is old. It is an *opaque* substance, and in its natural form its surface is rather *rough,* although for most uses it is first *smoothed* before being used.

D Suitable statements may be made in the following way, although these are models only.

1   Aluminium is ductile, light and a very good electrical conductor. It is also a very good thermal conductor and has very good corrosion resistance. It is soft and weak in its pure state. It is mostly extracted from bauxite.

2   Lead is a heavy, grey metal. It is weak and soft but has a high corrosion resistance. It is mostly obtained from lead sulphide (PbS), called galena.

3   Tin is an expensive metal. It is weak, but has a high corrosion resistance. It is mostly used as coating for other metals ('tin plate'), and is nearly always found as SnO_2 (cassiterite).

4   A mineral is a substance which occurs naturally in the earth. It often contains elements in compound form.

5   An ore is a mineral which contains a metal (or sometimes a non-metal, eg sulphur). It is used as a source for obtaining the metal.

E

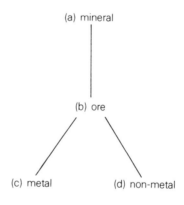

(a) mineral

(b) ore

(c) metal   (d) non-metal

drills

drill 1

The diagram shows a *pair* of vernier calipers, which can be used for the *measurement* of a *dimension*. The specimen *is placed* between the jaws, and the movable jaw *adjusted* until the specimen is just *held*. The movable jaw carries a vernier which moves over the *fixed scale*. The vernier is marked at *regular intervals* so that the fixed scale can be *further divided*. The vernier scale has a *total length* which is equal to one less than the *length* of a division of the *fixed scale*. The vernier has a length equal to *9/10* of each unit and is subdivided into *ten parts*.

drill 2

1	Hydrogen is inflammable.	true
2	Carbon dioxide is inflammable.	false
3	Carbon dioxide does not smell.	true
4	Ammonia is an acidic gas.	false
5	Carbon dioxide can be tested with litmus paper.	false
6	Ammonia is lighter than air.	true
7	Hydrogen is extremely light.	true
8	Oxygen can be used to put out fires.	false
9	Carbon dioxide can be used to put out fires.	true
10	Oxygen is used in making ammonia.	false
11	Carbon dioxide is less soluble than ammonia.	true
12	Ammonia has an extremely strong smell.	true
13	Carbon dioxide is heavier than all the other three gases.	true
14	Oxygen itself does not burn.	true
15	Hydrogen and air may explode.	true

drill 3

First, the two surfaces to be soldered should be thoroughly cleaned. The soldering iron should then be switched on and allowed to heat up. While it is heating up, the bit of the iron should be tinned. This is done by melting a small amount of solder which contains flux over the bit. When the iron has reached its working temperature, the surfaces to be joined should each be coated with a small amount of solder and flux. They are then placed in contact with each other, and the soldering iron is held against them while more solder is allowed to melt and flow over the join. The iron should then be removed, and the two components held together for a few moments until the solder has hardened. It is important not to try to speed up the cooling by blowing on the join. This may cause air bubbles to form in the join, and electrical and mechanical contact will therefore be poor.

The passage completed by the students should read:

Thoroughly *clean* the two surfaces to be soldered. *Switch* on the soldering iron and *allow* it to heat up. While it is heating up, *tin* the bit of the iron. *Do* this by melting a small amount of solder which contains flux over the bit. When the iron has reached its working temperature, *coat* the surfaces to be joined with a small amount of solder and flux. Then *place* them in contact with each other and *hold* the soldering iron against them. At the same time, *allow* more solder to melt and flow over the join.

Now *remove* the iron and *hold* the two components together for a few moments until the solder has hardened.

Do not try to speed up the cooling by blowing on the join. This may cause air bubbles to form in the join, and electrical and mechanical contact will therefore be poor.

drill 4

Soldering is a quick, simple method by means of which joints can be made between components made of steel, copper or brass. It is particularly useful in making wire connections in electrical work.

1   (b).
2   (c).

Good solder is soft and has a low melting point. It should therefore never be used to make a joint where strength is important or where it will be subjected to heat or vibration.

3   It is soft and has a low melting point.
4   Where strength is important or where it will be subjected to heat or vibration.

Solder is usually an alloy of tin and lead with a small amount of antimony. The melting point depends on the percentages of tin and lead present: the more tin there is, the lower the melting point will be, and the lower the strength of the resulting join.

5   (c).
6   (b).

Normally, solder is required to solidify quickly, but sometimes it is necessary to have a period when the solder remains soft while it is melting or solidifying. This type of solder must have a relatively high lead content—that is, about 70%.

7   (b).
8   The solder remains soft while it is melting or solidifying.

When making a join with solder, it is essential that the two surfaces which are to be joined are perfectly clean, otherwise the molten solder will not cover them completely. Without this coating of solder, the surfaces cannot be joined. A substance known as 'flux' must therefore be used to ensure the surfaces are clean and to enable the solder to flow over the surfaces.

9   Otherwise the molten solder will not cover them completely.
10 It ensures the surfaces are clean and enables the solder to flow over them.

drill 5

1 What's the difference between the density of lead and the density of gold?
   8,000 kilograms metres to the minus three.

2 What does the figure of 96 kilo Newtons millimetres to the minus two represent?
   The modulus of elasticity of copper.

3 Which has the higher density: copper or aluminium?
   Copper.

4 What is the modulus of elasticity of iron?
   205 kilo Newtons millimetres to the minus two.

5 Which has the lowest coefficient of linear expansion: aluminium, copper, gold or iron?
   Iron.

6 What substance has a density of 11,300 kilograms metres to the minus three?
   Lead.

7 Which substance has a coefficient of linear expansion of seventeen times ten to the minus six degrees centigrade to the minus one?
   Copper.

8 Which is the most-dense—aluminium, copper, gold, iron or lead?
   Gold.

9 What's the difference between the density of copper and aluminium?
   Six thousand two hundred kilograms metres to the minus three.

10 What's the modulus of elasticity of lead?
    Fifteen point seven kilo Newtons millimetres to the minus two.

11 Which substance has the highest coefficient of linear expansion?
    Mercury.

12 Which substance has a modulus of elasticity of 205 kilo Newtons millimetres to the minus two?
    Iron.

13 What does the figure of 8,900 kilograms metres to the minus three represent?
    The density of copper.

14 What does the value of twenty three times ten to the minus six degrees centigrade to the minus one represent?
    The coefficient of linear expansion of aluminium.

drill 6

1 What is the outer case made of?
   Metal.

2 What does the inner glass bottle rest on?
   A spring.

3 Where exactly is the vacuum in a 'vacuum flask'?
   Between the walls of the glass bottle.

4 What parts of the flask are silvered?
   The surfaces of the glass bottle.

148

5 What is used to seal the opening in the glass bottle.
A stopper.

6 What holds the stopper in position?
A screw top.

7 Does the glass bottle touch the sides of the outer case?
No, it doesn't.

8 What is placed over the top of the flask?
A cover.

9 Where is the insulating material positioned?
Between the metal case and the glass bottle.

activity

This may be handled in the same way as previous activities, with the class discussing the graphs together and making suggestions as to why they show certain features. This may be done by individual students being asked to suggest reasons, or by the class discussing possible reasons together.

The activity should include work on the two graphs separately, as well as a comparison between the two graphs and the demand for electricity in summer and winter.

Alternatively, the activity may be used as the basis for the testing of students' oral/aural skills. In this case, the teacher will need to see each student individually, apart from the rest of the class, and ask him or her a series of prepared questions about the graphs. The student should be asked, for instance, to describe the two graphs, account for certain features of them and to deduce features of the demand for electricity in winter and summer in the British Isles. When all the students have been interviewed, using a similar set of 'open-ended' questions, the teacher will be in a position to assess the relative abilities of the students in understanding and producing spoken English in a technical context in a controlled situation.